Lord from the Depths I Cry

A Study in the Book of Job

George M. Philip

First edition published 1986
by Nicholas Gray Publishing
26 Bothwell Street,
Glasgow G2 6PA

Scripture quotations, unless otherwise shown,
are from the New International Version.

ISBN 0 948643 00 5

Cover photo: Loch Tulla
Typeset by: Dove Typesetting & Printing Co. Ltd., Glasgow
Cover Design by Iain Love Graphics, Glasgow
Printed by Bell and Bain Ltd., Glasgow

Contents

Introduction to Didasko

One of the constant needs of the church, and a reiterated appeal from individual Christians today, is for *biblical teaching*. Does the Bible carry a message from God which speaks to us with relevance and power in these closing years of the twentieth century? Does it have something to say which will have practical repercussions in the lives of men and women and young people? If so, our first priority must be to grasp its message. The aim of the *Didasko* series of books is to meet this need through exposition of the books and fundamental doctrines of the Bible. *Didasko* is the New Testament's word for 'I teach'. We know from the New Testament that the basic element in the early church's teaching was the exposition of the Scriptures in a way that was clear, lively and Christ-centred. Precisely this is the purpose of all the writers who will share in this series of books.

Most, but not all, of the books in the *Didasko* Series are in the form of straightforward biblical exposition. They are not technical commentaries. Rather they explain the meaning of the biblical text and provide application of it to the Christian life. The contributors to this series are mainly men with considerable personal Christian experience and years of pastoral experience working with and helping Christians to understand the gospel more fully and to live in obedience to it.

It is the conviction of the publisher, contributors and the general editor of the *Didasko* Series that there is a great need for the kind of literature which this series represents. Their hope is that these books will contribute to meeting that need and will give instruction, challenge and encouragement to Christians throughout the world.

SINCLAIR B FERGUSON
Series Editor

Foreword

There are many mysteries about the Book of Job. We do not know when it was written, or where. We do not know who wrote it. All we really know about Job himself is found in the pages of this one book, together with passing references to him in Ezekiel 14:14 and James 5:11.

Yet, one thing is clear: the Book of Job is about *suffering*, and particularly about the suffering experienced by God's children. No book more clearly gives the lie to the superficial assumption that 'a little talk with Jesus makes it right, all right', for Job had to wrestle and struggle to the point of physical, mental, emotional and spiritual exhaustion before he even began to find true peace in his experience of suffering. That peace eventually came, not when he was able to understand his trials, but when he bowed to the sovereign majesty and grace of God. It was only when he was willing *not to understand*, that he began to understand. The narrative of his experience should teach us that life *is* not simple, and there is no 'simple' gospel which answers all of life's problems overnight.

The opening verses of Job stress the fact that he was a man of consistent faithfulness to God. Yet, he suffered to such an extent that all who knew him declared his godliness to be suspect. They accused him of secret sin, which he constantly denied. He refused to accept that this was the simple solution to his problems: sin brings suffering. He knew that *could* have been true. He believed that any man who is true to God will prosper. This was his dilemma. His basic creed: righteousness brings blessing, sin brings suffering, was shattered in his own life. He had been righteous, but he was suffering. He did not realise that there was another possible explanation — namely, that he was suffering, not at the hands of God, but in the hands of Satan; not because he was sinful, but precisely because he was righteous. Nor did Job realise that, in a very real sense, it was God as much as Job himself who was on trial. That trial, however, was taking place on earth — in Job.

Whenever, then, as far as you know your own heart, you are walking with God, and yet your life seems to be blasted by dark and evil powers, remember Job.

OUTLINE

SCENE SIX

EPILOGUE

The exposition of Job has been sub-divided in such a way that the book can be read through, or used as the basis for regular Bible study.

PROLOGUE
Chapters 1-2

Job 1-2
On Earth and in Heaven

1: 1-5

God chose Job for significant service in his kindom. He might well have said to him, 'What I am doing you do not understand now, but you will know after this' (John 13:7).

The story begins with the description of a godly man; then we are shown the heavenly scene where God challenges Satan (1:6-12); and then we see the blasting of the godly man's life with a sudden tragedy that is terribly grim. This process is repeated in chapter 2 and the saint is found in a hell of human distress that he could not understand. His pain is accentuated by the inhumanity of his so-called friends, with their rigid concepts of religion and the methods of God.

The rest of the book is the story of Job's wrestling in agony until at last he reaches the subdued peace of faith in the God whose ways, though past finding out, are ways of truth, righteousness and mercy. But remember that Job did not have the privilege of the knowledge given to us in the first two chapters. Look forward to chapter 23, and note especially verse 10: 'But he knows the way that I take; when he has tested me, I shall come forth as gold.' That is faith. When all around your soul gives way, when deep darkness hides the face of God from you and you lose all sense of his nearness and even of his existence, you are driven back in stark grim faith to say: 'Though he slay me, yet will I trust him' (Job 13:15). Do you trust God like that? Have you learned that he knows what he is doing with you?

Look carefully now at the description of Job. He was 'blameless' (v.1). His character was upright; his life was God-fearing; and his spirituality had a practical consequence: it led him to shun evil. The first verse speaks of integrity, maturity and reverence. In human terms he was well endowed, as verses 2-4 tell. But be careful not to covet prosperity, for it has a great capacity for deadening the spirit in a man. This man's consecration was so radical that God was able to trust him safely with the blessings of family, possessions, comfort and social prominence.

Verse 4 suggests a family who delighted in visiting each other in turn, although there may be a hint that they were more beguiled with material possessions than the father. Job was not deceived by their appearance, nor was he biased in their favour to the point of being blind to their faults, as parents can be. He knew he could not keep his children from living in the world; that would have created a spirit of rebellion against the 'holiness' and narrowness of their father. So he surrounded them by prayer continually. Parents, your children, out of love and respect for you, may behave at home, but unless they have a faith that is real, you will never know what they are doing when they are away. Better get down on your knees. That is better than nagging. It was Job's first concern.

1: 6-8

Events on earth can never be explained apart from the activity of heaven! We begin to see here that Job was to suffer just because he was the holy man he was, and because he was called and chosen for the privilege of this costly service. He did not fully understand, of course, but he was ready when God's time came.

The sons of God (v.6) are obviously angelic beings, the agents of God's administration on earth. Why then is Satan, the Adversary, found among them? He too, apparently, is the servant of God's purposes, being permitted to do his evil work in order to further the will of God. Some are willing servants of God, some are unwilling, but all must serve him. Of that there can be no doubt. Concerning these spiritual beings, compare Hebrews 1:14 and Jude 6. If they are here called to give periodic accounts of their activities, as these verses suggest, there is great comfort in Satan having to be present. Certainly there is nothing in the verses to indicate that his presence was surprising. Note very carefully in verse 7 that it is God who takes the initiative. He challenges the Devil.

But what is this going to bring to Job? From this heavenly standpoint, view your own life and weigh the issues of the coming days. What will they hold in the out-working of God's designs? You cannot take the risk of being out-of-sorts spiritually, not even for a moment. 'Be sober, be vigilant; because your adversary the devil walks about like a roaring lion seeking whom he may devour' (1 Pet. 5:8).

There are other things we must point out about Satan. He is a roaring lion. But here he is a slinking, evasive wretch. God asks where he has come from, not why he has come. Satan was *summoned*. Could it also be that God is rubbing in to Satan the fact that he is a fallen, discredited creature, subjected to a humiliating role because in his pride he sought to usurp God's throne? God is not afraid of the Devil.

Satan's answer is significant of the essential restlessness of evil. He was 'going to and fro' with no abiding place (v.7). Did he know he was serving God until God was ready to assign him to Hell? But Satan gives no real account of his doings. Nor can he claim significant victories in human lives against the grace of God.

Then God challenges (dare we say, taunts) Satan with one of his most glaring failures, a man called Job, of whom God is rightly proud, for he is the work of God's grace (*cf.* Eph. 2:6,7 and 3:10, to see God's deliberate purpose in saving and sanctifying sinners to make them a living demonstration, to men and angels and devils, of his glorious love and grace). God had a tremendous trust in Job. He knew his man!

1: 9-11

Cynical contempt is Satan's answer to the practical demonstration of grace in a human life: 'It is easy for Job to be good,' says Satan. 'He has all he needs, gets all he wants, is protected and prospered. It pays him to be good: but cross him once and you will see his true nature.'

Satan shows a very real understanding of human nature here, for it is in fact a good test of our religious profession when something jars and jags us. Can we take it? Many are proved to be lacking in real faith when the test comes. But Satan has no comprehension of what grace can do to a man's life. He will never give credit to a man for the transformation of attitude and character. He belittles everything you do and tries to get you to do the same to other people. Satan always slights, sneers and devalues. For example, when someone gives consistently and generously from their material possessions for the work of God, those of shallow satanic spirit comment contemptuously, 'He can afford it.' What a lie!

1: 12

Wait and see! That was God's answer to Satan's attack on Job. This is a frightening verse and gives a realistic emphasis to what we often say about God's ways being past finding out (Job 9:10). Within certain limits, permission is given to Satan to smite Job. We could compare this delivering of Job into the power of Satan with Jesus' experience (Lk. 22:53). He made it possible for men to do their worst.

But there is no question as to the ultimate issue, either with Jesus or with Job. God knows what he is doing. It is God's name and honour that are at stake. And furthermore, God's confidence in Job does not rest ultimately on Job's integrity, real though that is, but on his own grace and power which have made Job what he is (*cf.* 2 Cor. 12:7-10. God's strength is completed, fulfilled or shown most effectively in our weakness). There is no denial of our personality, nor any suggestion that we are robot-machines manipulated by God for his own ends. Have you never known the quickening of your natural talents and capacities, the emergence in crisis of a sharpness of mental activity, or the inflow of a peace that passes understanding, so that in hours of direst anguish you have experienced faith in a new way? That is the gift of the grace of God, and such a God would not fail his servant Job.

1: 13-19

We return from the heavenly viewpoint to the grim realities of earth to read of the swift tragedies that befell Job without the slightest warning. This was Job's evil day (Eph. 6:13). Note that there is nothing haphazard about this assault. Satan means business. In verses 16, 17 and 18 we have the phrase, 'while he was yet speaking,' which signifies successive, carefully timed attacks following upon the first assault.

Remember that all this is happening to a man of faith consistent in his spiritual life, living in a state of grace and under-girding his whole life and that of his children with earnest prayer. Does this mean our prayers for the safety and spiritual good of our people are in vain? Of course not! Would not Job often have prayed that God would make him a true and fruitful servant and use him for his glory? *Here is that prayer being answered.* I recall being counselled many years ago, 'Be careful what you pray for. You will get it.' When we give our lives to God, we assume it will be for service, but it may be for suffering or for sacrifice. Job was to suffer exceedingly; and his family died prematurely. These terrible tragedies came all in one day. We dare not minimise the cost and pain, but we dare not call it catastrophe. God is in this, therefore there is purpose and ultimately profit. This is how faith responds. Now read Romans 8:28 and see if you can believe it.

We are sometimes able to cope with even a terrible situation when it presents itself to us in distinctly spiritual terms and expressions. We know we are doing battle with spiritual issues and powers and our spiritual consciousness is alive to the challenge. But here it is different. The Sabeans (v.15) may have been natural enemies of Job's family for a long time, and an attack might have been overdue. It could have been seen as 'one of those things that just happens.' But Satan was in this and we need to recognise his influence.

The first messenger, carefully timed, is telling of a 'natural' hazard when another arrives to tell of 'fire from God'. Is that not meant to associate the first bad news with the action of God also? Then comes the report about the Chaldeans. Would you blame Job for thinking: 'Is God against me?' The Devil wants him to be in that state of mind when the report comes about his family. A 'great wind' is a natural calamity. It could happen anywhere to anyone. But Satan is buffeting Job's mind and emotions in order to shatter his trust in God, to sow doubt, to instil bitterness. Look at the repetition of the phrase 'to tell you' (vv. 15,16,17,19). It throbs with hellish persistence. It is like the pounding of our minds when we cannot sleep at night. There is no escape from it. The ruthless Accuser and Adversary is there. Beware!

1: 20-22

There seemed to be no escape for Job. Yet, look how he reacts. What a testimony to the depth and reality of his faith! His emotions are lacerated and his mind reeling, but he rises in full composure and dignity and in complete control of himself. Such is the inner discipline of his spiritual life that he is able to keep this shattering experience in perspective and he does what he always does, he worships before God in prayer. Job is teaching us a great lesson here.

Spiritual competence cannot be called out to meet a crisis unless it is first a basic part of normal life. Job here is a man humbling himself under the mighty hand of God (1 Pet. 5:6). He does not know whether God has sent this trial or permitted it, but he accepts it without resentment. There is no explanation, nothing but numb sorrow of heart. But in all this Job does not charge God with wrong (v.22).

Can we add to or elaborate Job's words in verse 22? He faces primary facts. He started with nothing; all he ever had came from God as an unmerited gift of grace; he has been allowed to keep these gifts for many years with pleasure and profit; has not God every right to withdraw them when and by whatever means he chooses? Job is not only saying God is just and right. He is confessing that God has been good to him. By such faith Satan is confounded.

2: 1-6

The first round of the heavenly war has been fought and won in the arena of Job's life and circumstances. Now the second round is about to start, involving Job's person, health and marriage. In and through the first blast of trial Job had not shifted his ground. He took his stand on the righteousness and love of God. Now a second 'evil day' is approaching.

We cannot tell whether or not there was much delay between the first two chapters. If some considerable time elapsed, as could well be the case, Satan would have waited to see if the unrelieved perplexity of Job's circumstances would break his faith and resolution. The absence of any word of explanation from God would heighten his anguish. Of course, God could not explain things yet because the battle was not over, and this particular work for God's glory had still to expand to its full manifestation. Job had to wait. This is why James speaks of

Job's perseverance (Jas. 5:11). He believed God knew best how to order the affairs of his saints. He did not pester God for explanations or solutions (*cf.* Heb. 10:35-39; 11:1,8,27 and 32-40; 2 Cor. 4:8-18). Although Job was not aware of it, God was using him in the mightiest spiritual service of his life! What a tragedy if Job, panicking away from faith, had contracted out!

On the other hand the time between the two chapters may have been short, and Satan may have pressed home his advantage. That seems true to his evil character. He prefers to strike us when we are down. But still the initiative is with God, as is made clear by God's boast in verse 3 to the effect that his man still stands fast. God is proud of his servant! Job will have his reward for this pain yet! God is no man's debtor. But Satan does not give in easily, and stung by defeat, perhaps incensed by the signs of ultimate defeat, his fury increases (Rev. 12:12). He sneers against faith, saying, 'Every man has his price. Touch Job in his own person and he will curse and renounce you to your face' (v.5).

Now, many a man will turn traitor to God rather than suffer pain or even discomfort. But it was not so with Job. Not merely his physical health but his mental health was attacked, as we shall see in succeeding chapters. The cruel, remorseless logic of his 'friends' became the weapon of the Devil, keeping up the pressure against the man of God. How long it all lasted we cannot say, but the fire proved Job's faith to be real, and reality stands firm.

2:7,8

These two verses should subdue a lot of our complaining about our human lot and make us ashamed of much of our self-pity regarding the costliness of true Christian living. It is all very well to sing about our times being in God's hands and our Father causing no needless tears, but when it comes to an actual situation like this, how would we fare? The precise nature of the illness is not important, but note how it embraced his whole body and reduced him to the most revolting condition, while he was fully conscious of all that was going on.

What were his thoughts? He had no idea what was happening to him, or why it was happening. Where was the God he trusted so implicitly with childlike faith in spite of all the grandeur of his social standing? To suffer and feel we are to blame is bearable, because there is an explanation. But to suffer when we are not aware of any cause in ourselves, *and* being aware that friend and foe alike believe that we deserve it and are paying the price of some secret folly — this is solitary agony.

Job was as a little child before God and he is seen as a bigger character than ever sitting amongst the ashes. In this respect Job was a true servant of the Lord, like Jesus (*cf.* Is. 53:37). You are in good company, Job. So are others like you.

2: 9,10

Job's patient endurance is here demonstrated in the face of the most poignant agony when his wife spat out her vicious words. She must have been amazingly insensitive to her husband's feelings before she allowed herself the satisfaction of this outburst. It seems she was far more concerned with herself, her own reactions and her social embarrassment, than with his need.

We recall that earlier in the story, while Job and his children are spoken of, there is no mention of his wife, nor of her sharing in the spiritual responsibilities of the family. We must not read too much into silence, but it does seem possible that she regarded her husband's function to be that of providing for her, not least in terms of social prestige. Now that Job was stricken they received few social invitations and little respect, since the commonly held view was that Job was suffering under the rebuke of God for secret sins. If Job had no resentment at God for his strange dealings, his wife certainly had. Her reaction was singularly unhelpful. To 'curse God and die' (v.9) is the last abandonment of faith and ushers you into bleak darkness.

Job's answer is surprisingly gentle in tone, though radical in content. He does not rail back at his wife, but confesses his continuing trust in the God who orders all his life righteously. He expresses disappointment with his wife, for he did not expect her to speak as a foolish or impious woman. Did he have a pang of doubt as to the spiritual rightness of his marriage? His wife completely failed to meet him at the point of his real need. Perhaps she did not understand or could not rise to the crisis. Was she then the right partner?

2: 11-13

We must be careful here to give Job's friends what credit is due to them. Job had been a man of prominence and many had been recipients of his kindness and generosity. Later, in chapters 29 and 30, we see how quickly their adulation turned to contempt. But there were three men who heard of Job's affliction and came to him with the avowed intent of comforting him by being with him in sympathy in his distress. When they came and were scarcely able to recognise Job because of his condition, they gave vent to their grief with all the gestures of eastern mourning. They did not have the heart to speak because they saw his grief was great. But did they not come to minister sympathy? It is never easy to speak true words of sympathy but it has to be done somehow. What held them back from speaking? Was it not the fact that they knew what they were going to say, words suggesting that the secret cause of distress was Job's sins and defective spiritual life before God? Was their seven days' silence a token of how grievous to them was their self-appointed task of 'dealing' with Job? There came a time when Job longed for them to be silent (*cf.* 13:5). But here it seems their silence was an added pain to Job, for 'after this' (3:1) Job bursts into intense speech.

Since we are at the threshold of the main section of the Book of Job, the long debate between Job and his 'friends', we do well to go back to the start to read through the first two chapters as a unit. This will set the stage for what follows. Unless we grasp the integrity of Job, his determination to stand by his claim to integrity, the confidence God has in Job, and the operations of the Devil, we will get completely lost in this book. The theme of the 'friends' is that Job suffers for his sins. Job agrees that he suffers, but insists that, whatever the cause may be, it is not punishment for secret sins.

The final accusation against the 'friends' is that their thoughts were rigid in their finality, no longer open to enlightenment. When they speak they are not warm with humanity but hot with indignation. Having known Job in earlier days they should have been slow to judge that he was now so utterly cast off. Their main failure, apart from failure to give tender compassion, was that they were utterly blind to the fact that this man was a servant of God. They were out of their depth and in their facile religious arrogance they fitted

Job into one of their text-book categories, and then set about him like devouring lions. Did we say lions? Yes. In the last analysis they are tools of the devouring lion called Satan.

SCENE ONE
Chapters 3-14

Job 3
The First Lament

Read the whole of chapter 3 to understand its torrent of words. Here is the man of God now attacked in his mind. There is a suggestion in the words 'After this' (v.1) that the silence of the friends and their manifest grief served only to accentuate in Job's mind the enormity and perplexity of his situation and condition. In chapter 1 Job coped with the loss of all he had, and remained composed in spirit. In chapter 2 when his body was smitten and his wife had broken under the strain, calling him to curse God, Job maintained the dignity and composure of faith. But now the tension of his mind is expressed in a flood of words. Remember that in a real sense the crisis is over for Job. The obvious attacks are over and the aftermath of emotional exhaustion and desolation has settled on the man. (Compare great Elijah's wail in 1 Kings 19:4, after his mighty victory on Mount Carmel).

Job's circumstances had robbed him of his sense of true dignity of personality. His awareness of the nausea of his condition dominated his consciousness. His whole mind was filled with his problem. His thoughts were absorbed, confused, racing, and non-productive, and all the time the tormenting thought persisted, 'God has forsaken you.' Little wonder Job broke into speech. Job's words got his friends speaking. That in turn led to wrestling discussion, and eventually to Job's words in chapter 19:25 — 'I know that my Redeemer lives'. By that time the Devil had overplayed his hand.

3: 1-10

While we seek to expose the work of the Devil, we should never make light of his craft and tenacity. Job here wishes he had never been born. But he had no choice in the matter, nor could he reverse the fact. The same principle holds regarding our conversion and call to service. We must obey. But what will such service cost? It appears that Satan does at times make a deliberate attack on our sanity. His aim is to immobilise the servants of God who would become the instruments of God in destroying the kingdom of evil. Evil is real; it is determined; it is destructive; it is personal, planned and operative among men. We need to take the whole armour of God and be prepared for battle like Job.

3: 11-19

Why, why, why? How often are we like Job, so utterly perplexed that we want to run away from it all. When Elijah asked God to take away his life, his prayer was refused because there remained a great sphere of fruitful service for him (1 Kings 19:10). It was the same with Job. He wished that he was dead and that all the past care lavished upon him had never been. Why? He felt he had lost God and that his life had no further useful purpose. He was wrong, of course. He was actually engaged in service, although he did not know it. He thought peace would come if only life would end there and then. But would peace be the inheritance, if we knew what our service might have been if only we had not panicked in the hour of trial?

Job had a well-formulated creed, but it was too rigid to contain the wise workings of the living God. The truth of God and about God is unchanging, but the methods of God have infinite variety. God fulfils himself in many ways. Dare we say that Job's cut-and-dried creed about how God dealt with his saints was shattered, and the final result brought Job to a new knowledge of the living, working, transcendent God? Peace is not the same thing as absence of conflict. Faith is not merely the acceptance of certain platitudes about God. Make sure you really believe in God and not just in your own ideas about God!

3: 20-26

Job speaks here in praise of death. His words sound strange

coming from the lips of a saint. His real perplexity is not the *fact* of his suffering, but the *significance* of it. If he could only see the meaning in it, all would be bearable, but instead there is simply wave after wave of restless trouble (v.26). He complains that his way is hidden (v.23), but the man of God must walk by faith and not sight. If there were never darkness, perplexity or trial, we would never learn faith; that is, we would never learn to translate our theological precepts into practical behaviour.

He says his way is 'hedged in' by God (v.23). Notice that Satan had said the same (1:10) but with a different slant. In any case, if Job believes his way is 'hedged in' *by God* should he not be at peace? But there is fear (v.25), a strange lurking apprehension from which he cannot escape. He cannot dismiss it, nor can he identify it. This is often a sign of Satan's work.

What is Job to do to gain peace? He must either banish his professed faith, exclude God from his reckoning and live like a beast for the pleasures of the moment, or he must include God and grapple his life to him with a desperate faith. This is what he does. So too, every Christian must expect and recognise satanic assaults so that they may be resisted. We are told in 1 Thessalonians 5:8 of the helmet which is the hope of salvation. That is not a pious hope that all may come right, but the sure and certain hope that all *is now* and *shall be* right, because the salvation of God is complete victory over every power and manifestation of evil.

Chapters 4-5
Eliphaz: Cold Logic

4: 1,2

Eliphaz is the first 'friend' to speak. He starts quite graciously, expressing a hope that Job will not be offended, and indicating that he feels led by God to speak. Eliphaz may have been mature in years (15:10). He delivers an impressive speech containing some wise truths (such as 5:17,18) and also some statements that cry out to be contradicted (such as 4:7). His discourse — scarcely the best technique of approach to a soul in deep distress — lasts until the end of chapter 5. Its theme is simply that all suffering comes from sin, and into this rigid concept of the working of God every individual case has to be fitted.

This is the blindness of spiritual pride, the arrogance of the over-confident, and the sin of those who are unteachable and thus incapable of recognising God. Because of this the Pharisees did not recognise the significance of Jesus nor did established Jewish religion recognise in the apostles the fulfilment of their own Old Testament Scriptures. Because it did not happen according to their preconceived notions of how God must work, they decided God was not in it. Here is a 'holy' man demonstrating both his blindness and his inhumanity. Be careful therefore before you pass judgment. Remember Isaiah 53:4b,5. Men saw a man cursed of God; God saw his appointed servant.

4:3-11

Eliphaz' theme is that God will always bless a good man and punish an evil man, and dispense his judgment swiftly.

Be quite clear that righteousness is rewarded and sin is punished. Never doubt that fact which underlies the moral government of the universe. But remember that there is mystery in God's forbearance with evil, and in his chastisement of the righteous. Remember that God has all eternity in which to punish evil-doers, while he has but a lifetime on earth to perfect his holy children in his service. In addition God has his unsearchable purposes, for the fulfilment of which he lays hold on his chosen men, calling them to suffer, as Christ suffered.

This kind of strong religion is not acceptable to Eliphaz. Was he jealous of Job's earlier prosperity, spiritually as well as materially? There is a sting in his words. 'You have helped a lot of folk, Job, but God has taken you down a peg now. Can you not take your own medicine? Tell me, when ever did the righteous suffer?' (v.7) We could trace the answer from Abel in the Book of Genesis to the martyrs in the Book of Revelation. Basic to Eliphaz' position is his own prosperity, from which he concludes that he is right with God. But many backsliders prosper materially, often because that is what they devote their energies to.

In verse 6 Eliphaz challenges Job as to his own beliefs. 'Should not your piety be your confidence and your blameless ways your hope?' Then follows the logical argument to prove that Job must be suffering for sin. But the methods of logic cannot explain the ways of God. Have you not found at times that you had no answer to people's words, yet you knew they were wrong? Leave them alone!

4: 12-16

Here is Eliphaz' real interest: his own subjective experience. What he claims is something which, by the nature of it, cannot be refuted. It was a private and secret experience, spoken about in order to give Eliphaz a superior position in argument. You cannot contradict a man when he claims this kind of thing, but you can query the nature of the experience. Such phenomena are not necessarily inspired by the good Spirit of God. There are many 'spiritistic' experiences, dreams, stirrings, movings, or leadings that are basically physical and emotional. They are 'soulish' rather than spiritual, and their carnal nature is manifested in pride and an unteachable spirit. Look how the man describes it. It was all very indeterminate and unidentifiable. His body trembled and his flesh crept. It was a sensuous experience, the memory of which remains in the forefront of Eliphaz' thoughts. That there are special experiences we cannot deny. Paul describes one in 2 Corinthians 12:1-10; but notice his reticence concerning it, refusing to make use of the experience in dealing with the Corinthians. The openness of worship in fellowship with believers taught in the Word is far safer ground than private flights of speculative experiences.

4: 17-21

Eliphaz' vision and voice spoke what was sound doctrine, held by many, including Job, who have never had the extra privilege of an 'experience'. 'Can a mortal be more righteous than God? Can a man be more pure than his Maker?' The answer is 'No,' and Job would be the first to confess it. The passage goes on to declare that if even the angels fall short, how much more do even the best of men.

The very wording of verses 19-21 would bring back to Job's memory the sudden snatching away of his children. What kind of comfort is this, telling a man things he has believed all his days, speaking them in conventional religious terminology? Where is the essential tenderness of spirit which alone ministers grace to the needy soul? Eliphaz is delivering a sermon that he considers rather a good one. But all the while he seems to be unaware of the bleeding heart of Job.

Job agrees with the doctrine, but it does not explain his situation, nor assuage his grief, nor bring light or peace to his heart. How easily we become 'Job's comforters'. This man has slighted Job's personal and spiritual character, exalted his own superiority and harrowed Job's heart with remembrance. But Eliphaz is only half done. Poor Job! Jesus would never treat you like that.

5: 1-7

Note the pattern of Eliphaz' dealings with Job the saint: first prolonged silence (2:13), then criticism (4:1-11), and then religious logic (4:17,5:7).

In this passage link 'fool' in verse 3 with 'his children' in verse 4 and you will see that the man is charging Job with the responsibility not only for his own condition but for the tragedy that befell his family. In verse 3 he is saying that he has watched men prospering outwardly but has discerned basic flaws in their lives and has known they would fall suddenly and disastrously. In verse 6 he says that affliction does not simply grow as weeds grow out of the dust, and in like manner trouble does not come to a man without there being a significant cause.

Verse 7 seems to mean that man's nature is to bring trouble on himself by his sin. Evil comes from his own nature like sparks from a flame (*cf.* Mark 7:20-23).

Eliphaz' broad doctrine is right, but in applying it strictly to Job he is prejudging the issue; he is wrong, because God is in this.

5:8-16

What spiritual arrogance Eliphaz shows when he says, 'If I were in your position, I would be crying aloud to God and seeking hard after him' (v.8). What does he think Job has been doing? If Eliphaz had been in Job's position (he never would be, he was not big enough or deep enough to enter into this kind of manly Christianity), he would probably have broken completely and cursed God to his face, like the many people who vow they will never darken the door of a church again because God has dealt with them in a way they do not understand. What they mean is that since God is not prepared to give them everything they want (as they may have done in spoiling their children), then they have no further place for him in the scheme of their lives.

In verse 9, Eliphaz is just mouthing a great truth. Of course God's ways are unsearchable and his methods past finding out and altogether different from ours. Why then was this man presuming to know so quickly exactly what God was doing with Job?

All this was sound doctrine to both Eliphaz and Job, but to relate the theory to the practical situation was beyond them. At least Job admits he is baffled. But not so Eliphaz. He does not have the spiritual calibre to reach the humility that acknowledges that God is bigger than his easily-held doctrinal basis.

Eliphaz! What has all your impressive sermon to do with Job? And what is it doing to Job, apart from impressing him with the hardness of your heart?

5: 17-27

Eliphaz is in full spate and we let him run on to the end, when he makes his final pronouncement, saying, 'That is my reading of the situation, my considered opinion based on the wealth of my experience. As far as I am concerned it fits the facts.' There is no sign of tears, as there was with Jesus when he wept over the sinful city of Jerusalem and grieved over the brokenness of men.

Oswald Chambers comments, 'It was this kind of pseudo-evangelism, so unlike the New Testament evangelism, that made Huxley say. "I object to Christians; they know too much about God." ' That was Eliphaz.

The difference between God's dealings, whether direct or by human instrumentality, and the dealings of men who are not moved by the Spirit of God is that God wounds *and in the process makes you whole.* When he makes you sore it is to bind you up, but men wound you and leave you with gaping sores and throbbing bruises. There is something quite demonic about man's inhumanity to man, and it is not lightly put right by sneaking up to the person you have hurt after many days or weeks, and with a watery, pious smile, acting as if all was well.

Eliphaz' swelling utterance is punctured by his own words in verse 21, for Job the righteous man, as we know from chapters 1, 2, was not spared the scourge of the tongue of the vain. It is all very well to discourse about the absence of fear, but it takes a deep spiritual character to be able to enjoy the table of God's bounty spread in the presence of your enemies (Ps. 23). This is not the blessing of the novice but of the mature, and maturity is gained at great price.

Job 6-7
The Soul's Dark Night

6: 1-14

Here is Job's reaction to the 'comfort' ministered to him. He was a man drawn into the mysterious workings of God, 'bearing the reproach of Christ' (Heb. 13:13 A.V.), and because the pattern of his life did not conform to the expectations of 'orthodox' belief, he was not recognised and was branded as a backslider. His 'friend' spoke many sound precepts, to which Job could give instant agreement. But Job needed real, not theoretical, comfort and his friend was being far too 'spiritual', churning out texts when tears were needed. Eliphaz probably never did one act of extravagant kindness all his life. Having been sound and true to the Word, he thought he had done rather well by Job, but in God's eyes he had failed.

In Job's reply there is a trace of sharpness or anger, and who can blame him? There is yet no triumph of faith, for he still wishes to die and thus resolve his perplexity (v.8). He says, 'What strength do I have that I should still hope? What prospects, that I should be patient?' (v.11). 'Do I have any power to help myself, now that success has been driven from me?' (v.13). Now ponder verse 14 deeply. 'A despairing man should have the devotion of his friends, even though he forsakes the fear of the Almighty.' Yes, even if he seems to lose all and breaks under the strain, gentleness, grace, tenderness and loving-kindness are still the first medicine in the cure.

This is Job's cry from the depths. From verse 4 Job defends himself and his deep melancholy. If there was not cause, he would not be crying aloud. He knows God is in his predicament, but why and to what purpose he cannot tell. It would be easy for Job to become morbid, to brood introspectively, seeking for extra sins to explain his experience. But deep in his heart he knows sin is not at the root of all this terrible conflict. The one thing Job cannot do is to be unreal, and therefore he has to grapple with the facts of his case until some gleam of light comes to him. He feels there is contradiction somewhere. He has not concealed or denied the words of the Lord nor has he disobeyed them. Yet he thinks God has smitten and cast him off. In fact God has committed the honour of his name to Job.

6: 15-30

Little wonder Job breaks out in this rebuke to his friends. When they came to him, of their own free will, they held out the promise of help: but in the reality of the situation they failed. Trouble often reveals your true friends and also their spiritual capacity. Job likens them in verses 15-20 to a stream that deceives. It is black and icy cold, swirling with concealed ice, dangerous and treacherous to the man who would travel on it. Again, it is like a stream that dries up in the heat, and the weary traveller who has depended on quenching his thirst there is frustrated.

Look at verse 20 and ponder it deeply in relation to your own ministry of care to your friends. Job is not sorry for himself; he is angry because his friends have added to the burden and agony of his situation by failing to recognise the basic sincerity and integrity of his soul. Love thinks no evil, but these men, as soon as they caught their first glimpse of Job's situation, gave it the worst possible construction. What a thing for friends to do! You see my predicament, says Job (v.21), and you are afraid: afraid for your own skins lest you get involved in something you do not understand in spite of all your pious words. These men failed in their understanding of what sympathy is. Do you know that the word 'sympathy' means literally 'to suffer together with'?

The exact meaning of these verses is difficult to ascertain, and you may benefit from reading various translations, although the essence of the passage is clear. In verses 22, 23 Job is either saying very pointedly that he did not ask them to come to him, or he is listing various common misdemeanours of public and business life. If it is the latter, he goes on to ask them to be specific in their accusations, so that he will know exactly which sin has caused the distress he now knows.

Look, says Job, you have uttered a spate of words, but what do they prove? You claim sincerity for your arguments, but you sweep away my desperate words as the utterances of a wind-bag (v.26). In verses 28-30 Job looks them in the face and protests his sincerity, pleads with them to return to trust in him for his righteousness in this matter. Does Job begin even now to see the significance of his plight? In the last verse he declares that he wants to be right as much as they do. If his sin has caused all this, he wants to be right even more than they want him to. But is it not likely that Job would have as good a palate for discerning the taste of evil as his friends? In terms of spiritual calibre, experience and fruit, these men had no right whatever to appoint themselves as Job's inquisitors. Be very careful if you ever take this role!

7: 1-10

Job now turns from his friends to God. His words are bitter and complaining, and yet are an appeal for compassion. Cast your mind back to the beginning of the story and remember that the silence of God throughout Job's trial stemmed from God's trust in his servant and in the issue of the work committed to him. Compare the silence of God at the time of the Cross. The Pharisees concluded that God had cast off Jesus (Matt. 27:43).

In v.1, Job's words compel us to do what we are so unwilling to do, namely, to ask ourselves what we are here on earth for. Job likens his experience to the labourer's longing for night and rest. But for him, months have dragged on, filled with apparently futile suffering. Nights are the worst, for there is no sleep. The struggle goes on ceaselessly (v.3).

Two things emerge here. Firstly, these are the words of a saint, for backsliders do not struggle, but usually lie in gross ease and complacency of spirit. Secondly, it is clear that the Devil's attack on this man is unabated. He is seeking to exhaust Job and at the same time is assailing his mind with

B

doubt as to the point of it all. Job is made to compare his days now with the earlier days when there were so many signs of God's blessing upon him. But visible appearances can be deceptive, very deceptive indeed.

Job is miserable because he feels that his day of service is past and that he will never be able to serve as he once did. Little wonder he found death so attractive a proposition! This is an example of the all-enveloping depressions that come from Satan. Job is 'begging God to ease him or end him' as Matthew Henry quaintly put it. The reason is that he feels himself like the weaver's shuttle cast swiftly backwards and forwards across the loom and now the thread has run out (v.6). Yet the product of the loom in the hands of a craftsman is not chaos, but a garment wisely and beautifully patterned.

Job was quite right about his swiftly passing days. If we had more sense of the brevity of our opportunity we would waste less time. But Job was wrong as to the product. The obverse or earthly side seemed a chaos of criss-crossing threads, but God saw the pattern emerging, and he was pleased with it. Life is not simple and we must learn to press deeply into God for its interpretation.

7: 11-21

Job's words are not a pattern of how to speak to God, but we may not adopt a superior spiritual attitude and criticise, for our circumstances have probably never brought us to this intensity of conflict. It may surprise some people to know that the saints at prayer are not always as serene as they are in a public prayer meeting. Agony can make you very incoherent in prayer (see Rom. 8:26). Job really feels life is virtually over for him, therefore he speaks as he does. He describes his awareness of an evil eye transfixing him and troubling him even to the extent of dreams and visions. But wait! Is this not an instance of Satan counterfeiting God with deeply moving 'spirtual' experiences? So successful is the tormentor that Job cries out *to God*, 'Leave me alone!' Mercifully God does not answer such prayers.

This word about Satan's wiles is important, for we forget his diabolical working at our peril. James Denney calls it 'the omnipresence, the steady persistent pressure, the sleepless malignity of the evil forces that beset man's life.' If you fail to reckon with Satan you will never understand your Christian life!

The merciless cruelty of Satan is seen in that he will give Job no peace even when he is asleep. But Job's words are being addressed to God when he says, 'Since I am such a wretched, worthless creature, why do you bother with me so long with visitations of trial? Give me up. Wash your hands of me.' (vv.16-19) 'What is man?' asks Job (v.17).

A good question! For he is *man* and not *beast*. That is why God takes such pains with the crown of his creation, for it is in man, fashioned and refashioned by gracious disciplines in costly service, that the glory of God is reflected in this world and the next. The glories of creation are wondrous, but it is in the grace of a Christlike life that God finds most pleasure. It is a great comfort to realise that God thinks us worth a lot of bother.

Job's words are wild because of his anguish. Paraphrase verse 20, 'If I have sinned, what harm have I done? You are too big, God, to be hurt by a puny man like me, and in any case, since I am a burden to you and to myself, why not be done with me?' But the last thing God wants is to be done with Job. God's honour is at stake in the face of Satan's accusations and that honour is in Job's safe-keeping. God knows his man.

Chapter 8
Bildad: Clinical Theology

8: 1-7

Bildad seems to break in here in impatience and exasperation with Job. The carefully enunciated precepts he declares mark him as an intellectual sadly lacking in humanity. He begins with a blasting rebuke and then goes on to propound a series of hypotheses: if . . . if . . . if (vv.4,5,6). To theorise about theology when a man is in agony of spirit is sheer cruelty. Remembering Job's recent bereavement, you see in the rough mention of the children (v.4), how indelicate Bildad is in both timing and method. It is clear that his concept of God is rigid. There is no room for the essential mystery of God. His ways are not our ways, but Bildad has the Almighty taped and pigeon-holed so that his actions can be predicted in any given set of circumstances.

Bildad's rebuke is based on the fact of the essential righteousness and judgment of God. But is there not an element of mercy, rather than harshness in God's righteousness? (See Ex. 20:6; Hos. 11:8,9; Luke 19:41). There is no sign of tears with Bildad. He is dealing with a 'case', giving the easy solution that all suffering comes directly from the sufferer's sin. It can be so, but often it is not. We have to seek a deeper answer here. Compare John 9:2,3 and 5:14 for two contrasting situations. Be careful before you judge or dare to give advice.

8: 8-22

Bildad is the kind of man who can beat you in argument, quoting all the appropriate texts and sayings of the fathers of former generations, and yet you feel instinctively that you are right and he is wrong. It is not as 'spiritual' as some people think to be able in a moment to give a cut-and-dried explanation of every perplexing situation. The true saint will often confess he does not understand the facts or the purpose of a situation and will give the counsel to 'wait upon God' until light comes. No such hesitation is here, alas.

Verses 8 and 10 together are wise counsel and many young folk would do well to submit their sometimes over-confident opinions to the sage advice of ripe experience. But in verse 9, far from admitting he is nothing, Bildad is actually slinging mud at the older man, glad, no doubt, to get the chance 'to take him down a peg.' If Bildad really meant, 'We are nothing,' both he and Job could have become scholars in God's school. But this man was unteachable. He knew it all; or so he thought.

The essence of the passage is simply, 'Where there's smoke, there's fire.' Therefore where a man like Job has crashed there must have been sin. Now we know that sin finds us out and may come home to roost after many long days. It is true that God will not cast off a godly man (v.20), nor ultimately prosper a wicked man. But these are final and eternal precepts, and in the present outworking amongst men of God's eternal righteousness, many strange manifestations of his permission and ordination are seen. Did not the Cross seem to be the casting away of the righteous and the triumph of the wicked?

The close of the chapter (vv.19-22) speaks of vindication from the God who turns our captivity, restores the years of apparent waste (and actual waste, though there is never excuse for wasteful backsliding) and gives a plentiful harvest in recompense for the tears of ploughing, harrowing, sowing and waiting (Ps. 126). Job believes the statement of verse 20 with all his heart: 'Surely, God does not reject a blameless man'. That is exactly why he cannot understand what is happening, for as far as he knows his own heart there is nothing between him and God.

Job 9—10
If Not God, Who?

9: 1, 2

With one question Job punctures Bildad's tidy theology. He points out that he has been preaching salvation by works on the basis that if a man is good God will bless, and if he is bad he will punish him. But the truth is that we never stand with God or deal with Him on a basis of merit, but only on the ground of grace. We must always acknowledge that at the best we are unprofitable servants. Any thought of holiness or desire to be good is there by the gift and work of his grace. We are nothing, have nothing, can do nothing and cannot be just with God. We have no ground on which to stand to plead a righteous case, and if we do battle of words with him in the court of judgment, we will not be able to answer one out of a thousand questions he will address to us.

Job stands on the same ground as Abraham in Genesis 18:25, where the holy man with great trepidation acknowledges he is but dust and ashes, and yet ventures to speak to the great God concerning his workings. Job is reaching that point here, recognising the vast majesty of God and the inscrutability of his wisdom and working, and seeing the need to humble himself under his mighty hand, that in due season God might do with him what he purposes (1 Pet. 5:6). Later we shall read Job's great affirmations of faith that shine as light in darkness. But this kind of faith comes out of the grim grappling with the facts of life and experience. There is no easy faith.

9: 1-24

This speech of Job's divides in two. Verses 1-16 discuss the relationship between a man and his God, while verses 17-24 constitute a bitter complaint by man against his God. The first section is the picture of man and God arguing the case in court. But God is far too big, and puny man quails before the manifestations of his grandeur and power. Later, in verse 33, we see Job's longing for an advocate to plead his case and to effect a reconciliation.

Christians have that advocate (1 John 2:1; John 14:16,17). Jesus speaks of 'another Advocate' besides himself, One who will be *in* us as well as *with* us. We have two advocates: the glorified Jesus with the Father, and the Spirit both within and around us. What a refuge in trouble and darkness! Jesus was the answer Job needed, and already there are gleams of that light in Job's darkness.

Job speaks here of a 'big' God who moves on in sovereign execution of his purposes. Man is very puny and it ill befits him to rail at God, even if he feels he is right with him. The words of vv.14-16 remind us to marvel more at the wonder of God's listening to and answering our prayers. We take it as a right, when it is a gift.

9:17-24

In this complaint of Job's we see the lie of the Devil that is at the heart of the man's anguish. He feels in verse 17 that all his toil is without purpose. Now, no man can continue patiently in bitter cost and suffering unless he is persuaded that good is going to result either for himself or others. But the 'fruit' of suffering is not always manifested in a way recognisable to us. Indeed, in Job's case, even at the end of the book, when his personal fortunes are restored, there is no earthly demonstration of the outcome of his suffering. The glorious triumph is celebrated in Heaven, in the presence of God and his angelic servants where Job's story began. What does this mean for us? Faith must believe that God is never wasteful in the sufferings of his servants. Whether we understand it or not, there is definite, creative, redeeming, sanctifying, God-glorifying, God-serving purpose and content in everything we are called to endure.

This is a far cry from Job's passionate outburst here as he pictures God hounding him and hurting him for no reasonable purpose. Job makes God out to be cruel and sadistic, refusing him a fair hearing, bewildering him with power, so that he would almost confess sins he did not really have in an attempt to get peace (vv.19-21). See Job's intensity (in vv.22-24) and hear his cry, 'If this is not God doing this, who is it?' Tell Job, and yourself, the answer 'It is Satan!'

9: 25-35

Here is desolation. In verse 24 Job says wickedness has triumphed. In verse 28 Job is afraid. In verse 29 he says, 'What's the use of trying, for (v.31) God pushes me back into the mire.' This is exactly Job's position now. He is fighting to believe in the perfect righteousness of a sovereign God, and at the same time is looking for a God human enough to come down beside him in his need. Verse 32 is almost as if Job was saying, 'If only I was dealing with a man who knew what it was like to be down here in this agony of life.'

Let us say again that only Jesus is the answer to Job.

The persistence of Job in wrestling with his grim situation signifies the presence of faith. This is why battered Christians come back to fight again. It is their true nature, though they may not understand why or what they are doing. They go on because they must.

Job recognises that since God is not a mere man to be argued with as two lawyers of equal status argue in a court, there needs to be someone to stand between him and this great God, to effect a righteous reconciliation. Job mourns because there is no such mediator. Again we must go to the New Testament to find the true facts. There is a Mediator — he is 'the *Man* Christ Jesus' (1 Tim. 2:5).

In verse 34 the gleam of hope has faded and Job is left alone with his suffering. Still he clings to the fact of his integrity, as opposed to the accusations of men and devils. If God would only take away his rod, and ease his paralysed spirit, Job would speak with him and not fear; for deep within himself he is not afraid of God. That seems to be the sense of the last verse. Job is quite right. You can speak with God when you have a conscience void of offence. Note that in spite of depression Job still knows that his final solution lies in getting *to* God and not in running *away from* God. Is there not something to be learned here concerning the reality of our profession of faith?

10: 1-16

'I will give full expression to my complaint' (v.1). Job says to God, 'Tell me what is wrong' (v.2). The man is full of questions. Is this all God wants of him, to shame and confound him (v.3)? Verses 4-6 seem to suggest that God is short-sighted like men, working from day to day with no long-term purpose and content simply to ferret out sin, and punish it swiftly without true examination of the case. But God must know that Job wants to be right and is in fact right (v.7). Is it then a waste of time trying to be right with God and ordering your life with care as Job did? Think back to chapter 1 and the description of Job's spiritual and moral integrity.

Job has reached the stage of saying, 'What's the use of going on?' but in the very moment of thinking such a thought he speaks wonderful truth in verse 8. Faith discerns a contradiction in the tumult of thinking. God's hands took pains with him, fashioning him with care. How can that same God intend destroying him? Does God just pick up a man to cast him down again like a child who has wearied of a toy? Of course not. Granted God's ways are mysterious but they are not fickle. He knows exactly what he is doing and his methods have divine accuracy. Real faith believes that God is working *everything* together for the good of those who love him (Rom. 8:28), in spite of immediate appearances. So does Job later, in 13:15.

Job is speaking to the Great Potter (*cf.* Jer. 18:1-6). In verses 8-12 he looks back to before he was born and traces down through the years the evidences of the creative hand of God making him what he is. Look at the magnificence of Job's testimony in verse 12. This is what Job knows as he looks back over his life. He knows he responded wholeheartedly to the loving-kindness of God. But now, Satan has injected doubts about God into his thoughts and feelings.

But Job, you cannot have it both ways! *Either* God is the great and gracious Potter fashioning the hand-made, heart-planned vessel for his pleasure and purpose, *or* he is a petty tyrant, false and perverse, leading you on for the sheer pleasure of enjoying your collapse.

Job says he is confused, and little wonder, for he has listened to the lies of the Devil in the speech of his 'friends'. He thinks of a God who is bent on marking every minute transgression. But it is not God who is the roaring lion (1 Pet. 5:8). Here is the Accuser and tormentor seeking to move Job from the ground of his integrity in order to destroy his fruitful service. The same policy of the Devil operates in our case to keep us from reckoning on our position in Christ. We are being shown Job's experience to understand our own.

10: 17-22

Look at the deep cry of perplexity and despair in verse 18. 'Why has this to be?' pleads Job. It is going on so long. He is brought so low and kept there by recurring surges of battle until he is weary and quite worn out. It would be a relief to die. Verse 20 breaks the heart, as he pleads for a few days of quietness before the final silence of the grave. But the battle is not over, and the continued malice of men is the spur that drives Job on until chapter 19:23-27 when even the grave is bright with light.

Job's persecutors are guilty men, but God brings good out of their evil, just as God overrules even our own sins. Here Job can see no way out of his plight and failure, and his wistful words are full of tears. A few verses later we find his next friend whipping him with words. But let us first take a biblical example of the attitude of God in a case like this, so that we may learn the compassionate ministry of care.

Turn to 1 Kings 19:1-8. Elijah, prophet of fire and deep sensitivity, all alone, deep in a sense of failure, is cradled to sleep by God and ministered to until his strength has returned. Then, and only then, is his instruction resumed. There is no substitute for genuine compassion — like God's.

Job 11
Zophar: Merciless Preaching

11: 1-20

There may be some truth in Zophar's sermon to Job, but there is certainly no humanity in it, and remember it is spoken to a man of ripe years whose heart has been laid bare by suffering. Job's friends are annoyed with him because he will not accept their interpretation of his life, and Zophar reacts with a show of righteous indignation. Zophar is so inflamed by Job's claim to righteousness that he invokes the blast of the Almighty's word against him. Note how these friends of Job's have a deep contempt for his knowledge and experience of God. It could well be that in past days they envied Job his spiritual standing and fruit, and now are secretly delighted that he has struck a bad patch. They are determined to make the most of it. How true to human nature!

Verse 6b is a glorious utterance in general terms. But Job had already consented to this glorious doctrine and yielded to it in worship in chapter 1:20-22; 2:9,10! Zophar would have been on far truer spiritual ground if he had admitted he did not understand what God was doing with Job. His words display his ignorance.

Job, though much perplexed, was certainly nearer a true apprehension of the bigness of God and the mystery of his working than was Zophar, with his tabulated, text-book theology. It is easy to throw in a few texts as your contribution to a discussion about life, but verbal gymnastics never come near the heart of the mystery of human experience. In verse 10, Zophar says God can do what he likes. We agree, as does Job, who has already spoken of the absolute sovereignty of God (9:1-12); but that does not answer Job's present perplexity nor does it bring him comfort. Zophar is telling Job he cannot hide from God, failing to see that far from hiding from God, Job wants to come near to God to see him face to face.

Apart from truth being learned in these readings, is it not a thrill to see Job towering in stature over these religious pygmies? This is the fruit of a man who knows what it is to bow before God in worship. The veiled accusations of guilt from his 'friends' have moved Job to indignation and he will now answer them to their faces.

Job 12-14
Struggles in the Dark

12: 1-12

Job begins his answer with a blistering attack on his friends' arrogance, and climaxes it in chapter 13:5 with an equally pungent comment to the effect that they might pass for wise men if they learned to keep their mouths shut. This is not an 'un-christian' attitude and sentiment, but the necessary demolition of untried and youthful novices who have the temerity to 'talk down' to a man of Job's calibre and experience. Like some Christians, they thought they knew everything there was to know about God and his workings among men. Such persons are raw in experience and should wait to demonstrate their competence in running their own lives and their careers before they presume to tell others how to do so!

Job stabs at their conceit, saying that no doubt they were the only wise people in the world and when they were dead no one would know anything about God because wisdom would die with them. Some arrogant egotists are amazed when a piece of Christian work does not collapse when they abandon it. They might be surprised how little their departure is noticed. The common-place truths they are mouthing so sanctimoniously are generally accepted, but such adolescent attitudes do not face up to the mysteries of actual experience. You must discriminate and discern (v.11) and refuse to judge by superficial appearances. But that requires the grace of humility to confess many a time that you are baffled. One commentary on Job is entitled, *Baffled to Fight Better*.

Job goes on to speak of God the universal Lord, present and operative in every aspect of his creation. But how many Christians have eyes to see and hearts to believe? Look out through the world. Do you see your God at work? Does he give you peace? The issues belong to him, as do the methods and processes of their outworking. Fear him, and you will then have nothing else to fear.

12: 13-25

Job's concept of God is that of a personal God, working by his own power and authority, yet working with reasonableness according to plan. God is not capricious or haphazard. His every work is deliberate, with nothing incidental or accidental. He is a cosmic God, working by sovereign power without human aid, yet pleased to work by human instruments, in every sphere of world activity.

Look at what Job says in verses 14, 16 and 23. Do you believe in a real God like that? Do you realise that this God is presently at work in the affairs of men, in your city, congregation, family and personal life? Have you learned to wait upon God so that you may know the significance of his ways with you? Or, have you reduced God to a few theological propositions as Job's friends did, so that you escape the costly travail of coming to grips with the realities of life? Is your God big enough to enable you to look squarely at the baffling inconsistencies and paradoxes of experience in a way that enables you, indeed compels you, to worship? The following passages provide the framework of a Bible Study on this theme: 2 Thessalonians 2:7-12; Romans 11:33; Acts 17:24-28; Habakkuk 1:5,6,11; Psalm 139; Isaiah 45:5-7,15,18,20-22; Daniel 4:17; Isaiah 55:8,9; Zechariah 2:13; Habakkuk 2:20.

13: 1-13

Job is tired of the easy words and glib answers trotted out by his friends. There is nothing quite so nauseating as the prattle of those who talk as if they know all there is to know about God. That is indicative of nothing but spiritual pride and shallowness of both character and intellect. When such people cannot make you succumb to the pattern of their theology, they get angry and write you off as a backslider. They need to be told: 'Keep silent!' (v.13).

Job wants to reason with God in order that God should explain the conflict between what Job believed about him and what he was now experiencing. Job believed God is, and that he rewards those that seek him (Heb. 11:6). Well, Job was seeking God with all his heart, but what kind of reward was this? Was God being unrighteous?

In order to protect God's integrity, Job's friends were forced to attribute sin to Job. They were justifying God's actions (v.8). These men were being unjust to the facts of Job's situation in order to keep in with God! But God is no respector of persons and will expose the inconsistencies of any man or group of men. He is concerned with the truth every time. 'You who make such a boast of the sovereignty of God and his all-searching eye, remember he looks upon you and, if he finds you dabbling in untruth, he will confound you. Hold your peace!' says Job. He stands by his convictions and is prepared to pay the price. Time will tell if his trust in God and his integrity are well founded or not.

13: 14-19

Job knows he can trust God and will trust him even if his present situation results in death. But Job knows he will yet be vindicated (v.18).

He does not know what God is doing with him, but he knows in his own spirit that the explanation does not lie in his sins. Job is not claiming sinlessness. He is too real for that. But, having set his heart to seek after the Lord, he knows he is accepted. He knows God is doing *something* with him; but *what it is* Job does not know, nor can he explain to the bickering questionings of his friends. But his trust in God is unreserved. Even if God's plan is to erase him from life, even if that is all God has made him for, just to kill him in this most painful manner, then let God be God and his will be determinative. 'I will still trust him,' says Job. 'I know whom I have believed, and see no reason to reverse my committal to him. Though he slay me, yet will I trust him.'

13: 20-28

What a glimpse we have here of the tender heart of Job, and

with what poignant words he addresses God in prayer. He says, 'Do only two things for me.' What are the two things? He pleads for the removal of outward pain and inward dread. These two heavy weights on Job's spirit are making any true communion with God virtually impossible, and it is while under this cloud of weary depression and dread that Job utters the extreme and bitter words of the last few verses of the chapter.

One of our hyms says, 'They who fain would serve Thee best are conscious most of wrong within.' That is very true, and naturally so, for as we draw nearer to the Lord, the light of his presence shows up the shadows and stains in our lives. But the Devil seeks to use this sense of unworthiness to bring us into such a bondage of guilt that we cease to be of any use to God at all. Job here could think of many reasons why God should punish and desert him, but still his one desire was to speak with God.

Job's heart-cry reaches breaking point in verse 24. God was hiding his face from him but it was a satanic suggestion that God held Job as an enemy. When the blackness settles on our souls in this total way, and there is no answer to the heart-cries of earnest desire to God, we can be sure that Satan is at work with his accusations and lies, seeking to stir basic doubts in our souls about God.

But where is God and where are all his promises of victory? He is allowing you to plumb the depths of trial to prove to you how total is the victory he can give you. Faith trusts in the dark even when it cannot see.

14: 1-22

This is a dark and dismal chapter with but few gleams of light and hope as Job wrestles with the grim facts of his experience. Here he is, a man stripped of all the externals and incidentals of life. He has been reduced to rock-bottom, until he is just a body of painful flesh, gasping for breath, with his mind racing with questioning thoughts. Yet he still believes in a good God and feels there must be more to life and experience than this awful shambles of suffering. He is getting to the stage of saying, almost in defiance of his circumstances, that *all this is not for nothing.*

He is quite right. Every painful throb of body and mind is

fraught with significance in the purposes of God, and is in fact, while the struggle is still going on, declaring the triumph of the grace of God in human life.

Job is nowhere near such a well-defined interpretation of his experience yet, but is struggling on towards it. In verses 1,2,5,10 and 12 we have Job's thoughts of life and death. Life seems so short and painful, and death so callous and final. Job seems to see the trees in a better situation than men. The tree felled may yet bud again if the root remains, for it draws life from a source deeper than immediate appearances show. If it is thus with the trees, can God have less in his plan for men? Death cannot have the last word.

'If a man dies, will he live again?' (v.14). This is the ultimate issue for Job. He wants to relate his present life to that after death. If he were sure of the life to come he would be prepared to suffer in this life right to the end. The explanations could come afterwards.

But almost at once Job falls back into a dread sense of God as a grim, relentless judge set on breaking him. God is the Mighty One whose power pulverises the works of nature and destroys the hopes of men. Death finally seems to gloat in triumph, cutting man off from all that is dear to him. To crown it all, he seems to feel there will be no end to his pain even in death (vv. 16-22).

What a darkness there is in such thoughts of death apart from Christ. This is what is meant by the phrase 'a Christless grave.' But how many live and die without Christ and without hope! There is no excuse, for the full light of hope has shone before men's faces in the person of Jesus.

SCENE TWO
Chapters 15-21

Job 15
Eliphaz: Words of Rebuke

15: 1-16

The sequence of speeches and answers now begins again. But there is one difference. Having listened to Job's words, his friends now manifest even less sympathy than before and much more sharp criticism. Job wrestles with a great intellectual struggle that is yet to bring him to faith's triumph, but his friends speak from the static position of creed, coupled with emotional exasperation with a man they are too small to understand. One cannot help thinking that there was in Job's 'friends' some jealousy or grudge against him that gave such persistence to their malicious criticism. Of course, they would deny this, and claim to be speaking on a 'spiritual' level.

It may be that they were conscious of not getting the best of the theological argument, and true to human nature they shifted their ground and attacked the man. One commentator says Eliphaz is, 'Saying nothing with terrific emphasis.' One thing is certain: the spirit manifested in these opening words is so devoid of grace that you can be sure the rest of the speech will accomplish nothing but a great demonstration of the spiritual emptiness of Eliphaz. He is too big in his own eyes. What a contemptible character this man is. 'Who do you think *you* are?' he asks Job with a sneer. 'All *the best people* agree with us.'

You can imagine Job replying that all the best people are as wrong as Eliphaz is! This man does not reason, but pours abuse and scorn on a suffering man. Whatever else this is, it does not betoken bigness of character, let alone spiritual depth and understanding. Look at verse 8. Eliphaz knows nothing of the secret counsels of God, else he would understand the significance of saintly Job's sufferings. Further, Job has been professing his failure to understand all along, and can hardly be accused of limiting wisdom to himself. Look at the childishness of verse 9, as a grown man mouths the words of pettiness, 'We are as good as you, anyway.' How can he speak of the consolations of God (meaning the sermons earlier hurled at Job)? In verse 14, 'What is man?' is a final sneer at Job. But look on to verse 17 and you find 'I' twice and 'me' twice out of seventeen words. That tells all!

15: 17-35

When Eliphaz said in verse 14, 'What is man?' he was only concerned with demolishing Job and rubbing his nose in the dust. This heartless attitude of contempt was typical of Eliphaz' attitude to men. They were but the tools of his theological trade, souls to be dealt with, or spiritual scalps to be added to his belt to display his spiritual prowess. That is why in this section we find him able to declaim about judgment, describing the fate of the wicked as if he were shouting the selling price of cattle for slaughter.

We do not contradict his words about the final judgment of the unrepentant wicked, but we do query the spirit that motivates the sermon. Any man faced with the grimness of suffering humanity who can utter words of unrelieved judgment like this, without the trace of a tear of compassion, is utterly different from the man Christ Jesus who wept over the city that was doomed. The aim of the sermon is clear. It is to point to Job and say, 'Thou art the man!' These ardent 'holy' men, who had a great nose for others' sins, were determined to make Job confess to sins that he did not have. Had Job yielded to their accusations, he would have ended in a deep satanic bondage which would have destroyed his mind as well as his psychological balance. Stick to the facts and wait for God to interpret them!

Eliphaz is beating his usual drum about the wicked suffering for sin. But this is true only in the ultimate analysis.

In this life God is more concerned to deal with his own saints, for while there is loss as well as reward in Heaven, there is neither punishment nor refining. The time for preparation is over and the saints have entered their eternal service. It is then that God can turn his undivided attention to the punishment of the wicked. This means that right through life the wicked may well prosper and enjoy his sinning. Look around you and you will see plenty evidence. The wicked are reserved for judgment (2 Pet. 2:4,17; 3:7). Their foot shall slip *in due time* (Deut. 32:35).

By contrast, true faith finds no perverse pleasure in the fate of the wicked. Nor does it become despondent at evil's arrogant display. Faith waits to the end through thick and thin. Weak faith clamours for immediate explanations and solutions. Strong faith is given the privilege of walking in the dark. This is Job's story and the 'holy' sermonising of Eliphaz is but the yapping of hell, seeking to panic the man out of God's work. But Job is even now beginning to feel more and more that there is a work of God going on and he refuses to come down. Indeed he is about to give the curs of hell rather a fright!

Job 16-17
Can This Be God?

16: 1-5

Aren't you glad Job gets the chance to speak these words? They are not likely to make his 'friends' more benevolent towards him. But friendship can never be founded on pious twaddle, only on reality and truth. Some have few friends because they are not prepared to deal on a basis of what they really are. They act a spiritual part and all their associations almost become part of a game.

How many 'miserable comforters' give you a sermon when a word of human kindness is what you really need! It would not have been so bad if these men had had some new facet of God's truth to pass on, although even then sound theology is no substitute for care.

Job's agony is leading him on to a spiritual level where the arrows of men can no longer pierce him, though they may still distress him. He marvels in verse 3 at the impudence of these men in so railing at a man whose fruitful life was factually and statistically beyond question. Their words were empty. May God save us from becoming such windbags!

Job counsels his friends to consider what might happen if the tables were turned. He could tell them a few home-truths about themselves, but he would rather use his energies in ministering strengthening care. When a man's life is groaning in brokenness it is seldom then that God would have us administer searching rebuke. At times that is the necessary treatment to produce a cure. But even then it must be administered with exquisite care and gentleness which, while it in no wise blunts the healing edge of truth, yet brings comfort to the wounds. Those who most resist every attempt to minister to themselves often become the harshest to the fallen. Beware!

16: 6-17

In this passage which reveals the intensity of Job's suffering, about whom is he speaking? Is it God? Or Job's friends? Or is the enemy some other 'character' not yet clearly defined in the story of Job's experiences? He begins by saying there is no change in his condition whether he speaks (expressing his feelings in words or prayer) or keeps it all within himself. He is quite clear that whatever is happening it is not punishment for sin (v.17). Is his enemy man or God? Is God *permitting* all this or is he *ordaining* it? Do you not want to shout out, 'Job, there is a Devil behind all this!'

Have you ever felt like this? What must you do? Fight your way through, by faith, until you grasp the twin facts of God and Satan, for only then will you understand men. But remember, the initiative is always with God. Now, do you begin to understand your life as a Christian? If you have no such conflicts as these, it may be because you are safely asleep in the Devil's arms.

16: 18-22

What an honest book the Bible is! It displays the humanity of the saints, their high peaks followed in a moment by plunges into irrational doubt and despair, in which they contradict spiritual truths they earlier affirmed for their comfort. Compare verse 22 with chapter 14:14 where Job glimpses in life beyond the grave redress and explanation of his present conflict. Here his heart is more gloomy, as he thinks of himself drifting off the scene to be forgotten.

Job pleads that nothing may be allowed to silence his cry to God. He expresses a longing that there might be someone to plead for man with God on a basis of neighbourliness or friendship (v.21). The glory of the gospel is that there is such a One. His name is Jesus. But Job does not know this. He falls back into the gloom of doubt again, for he feels he will not last out long enough to prove his innocence and victory.

Later in this book we find Job able to defy even death and the disintegration of his body into dust. But even here we see a man who is persuaded that there is an unseen Witness in the shadows keeping guard over his own with a heart of wonderful compassion. Job maintains a stern composure and dignity before scornful men; but he knows it is safe to let God see his tears. This is the God Job knows and trusts. This is the God who takes Job's side. But Job's friends are on another's side. They are against God's man. That is a bad state to be in, and very dangerous.

17: 1-5

Job now lapses into dark despair, partly because he had looked to his friends for understanding and had found none, and partly because he had looked to God for some vindicating or confirmatory sign and had not received it. In verses 4 and 5 Job's anger at his friends begins to turn to pity, for he sees that wrong men are in the hands of God as well as right men, and God will requite them. To 'denounce' (v.5) or pronounce verdicts in the midst of sore suffering is an evil occupation, and God will not hold you guiltless if you indulge in it.

Job appeals to God: 'My spirit is broken; my days are cut short; the grave awaits me' (v.1). Wherever he looks he sees continued mockery and criticism. He asks God for a sign or token of vindication so that he will know God acknowledges his innocence before he dies (v.3). But Job already had such a token — the witness of the Holy Spirit within his own heart to the effect that he knew he was basically right with God. He expressed it in chapter 16:17. But the fight of faith can last a long time; the Scriptures teach us that we must labour to enter into the rest of faith: Hebrews 4:11; 10:35,36; 11:13. What faith — to die with nothing but a promise to rest on! But the promise is sure.

17: 6-16

Job makes no attempt to hide his distress. In verses 6-9 he says that all the 'best' people stand aloof from him, making quite clear that he is under censure.

In verses 10-16 it seems that hopelessness is closing in on

him, and this highlights the cruelty of the next speech of Bildad (19:15,19). Remember that Job was suffering all this because he was a man drawn into the secret and eternal purposes of God's righteousness. This will help you to understand a little of what Jesus felt and knew when he prayed in the Garden that the particular cup of suffering might be taken from him. You will then sense a new depth of awe every time you read the Saviour's words from the Cross, 'My God, My God, why have you forsaken me?' There was no answering voice from heaven. The agony had to be. It was so also with Job.

We could pause at this point to consider what spell of time has so far been covered by Job's experiences. We cannot really tell. In 1:6 reference is made to 'a day'. In 2:1, 'Again there was a day.' In 2:13 seven days are reckoned. In 3:1 the narrative continues, 'After this.' The span of time could be short or long, but we favour the long, for the passing of many days would accentuate and add to the cost of Job's suffering. Sudden crisis can teach many lessons, but the passing of time drives the lessons home, deep into the soul. Consider Abraham's thirteen barren years (Gen. 16: 16-17:1); the long years it took to bring Jacob to Peniel where he became a broken and fruitful man (Gen. 32:24-32); the years of Joseph in Egypt; Moses in the desert forty years; Paul in Arabia fifteen years; John in lonely exile in Patmos. Whether in us or through us, God works on a long-term policy that both evil and righteousness may work themselves out to the full, the one being brought to judgment by the other.

We must not weary. This may be evil's hour, but to those who stand in the evil day victory is absolute certainty, as is glory.

Job 18
Bildad: Words of Anger

18: 1-21

Bildad is angry with Job because of the pointed things said about his wisdom, spirituality and character in chapter 16:1-5. This anger is expressed in a chapter that burns with cruelty as he seeks to thrash Job with words of spite. Bildad's spiritual 'superiority' has nothing in it of the love that suffers long and is kind. But then, many 'holy' people show another side to their personalities when they are crossed or criticised. Bildad is puzzled by Job's experience and perhaps a little frightened by its dimensions. It is not easy to face what is apparently the triumph of evil in a good man's life and relate it all to the righteousness of God. But the answer is certainly not to shout and criticise the suffering man who is faced with and frightened by the same mystery of evil.

Bildad describes the character, attitude and fate of the worst man he can think of and applies it all to Job. If Job would only confess to some sin or wrong in his life, then there would be an explanation of the situation and Bildad's theology would be nice and tidy again, with all the easy answers neatly pigeon-holed ready for the next case to be dealt with. This is comfortable religion. Its defect is that it is not true to life, to man or to God. It is certainly not true to the Devil.

In verse 4 Bildad may be addressing his companions in Job's presence, or saying directly to Job, 'You are tearing yourself in anger. Has the whole world to adjust for your sake?' The contempt and anger cannot be concealed and the aim is to hurt, demoralise and get vengeance for what Job has said. This is a satanic response and a continuation of the spiritual assault on God's saint. It is not the first time that religious men have done Devil's work in the name of God and religion. This man is so angry he cannot possibly see things in true perspective. He is blinded by the 'hurt' that has been done to him.

Admittedly Job's words were very pointed, but he was under tremendous spiritual pressure at the time. Should the 'strong' Bildad not have made allowances for the 'weak' Job? Is it not the privilege and duty of the 'strong and advanced Christian' to become the servant of the weak and faltering, to encourage and lift up rather than to administer the final blow that will crush? Bildad was not a right man. He failed to see that the holy work of God with the reputation of God was in Job's safe keeping, not his.

Job 19
God Invisible, But Real

19: 1-12

Job can no longer contain himself as he listens to Bildad, and he bursts in and pleads to be left alone. He asks if they have no heart at all (v.3). Can they not see that if he has sinned then the remembrance of it would be with him now (v.4), for he has cried to God to search him? Now Job knows God is in this situation somewhere, doing something, but he cannot fathom it. He would have been shocked into worship if he had known just then *how much* God was doing through him, and *on what dimension* this work was to be evaluated. Look at verses 9-12 and think of the many hymns that speak of such experiences:

When all around my soul gives way,
He then is all my hope and stay.

When we in darkness walk,
Nor feel the heavenly flame,
Then is the time to trust our God,
And rest upon his Name.

Workman of God! O lose not heart,
But learn what God is like . . .

> *Thrice blest is he to whom is given*
>   *The instinct that can tell*
> *That God is on the field when he*
>   *Is most invisible . . .*
>
> *He is least seen when all the powers*
>   *Of ill are most abroad.*
>
> *God moves in a mysterious way,*
>   *His wonders to perform . . .*
>
> *Judge not the Lord by feeble sense,*
>   *But trust Him for His grace . . .*
>
> *God is His own interpreter,*
>   *And He will make it plain.*

19: 13-22

There is a particular agony in being alone and in feeling deserted in a time of crisis and distress. It is almost too painful to read these verses, let alone try to apply them. Have you ever experienced this kind of torture: the aloofness of erstwhile associates, the contempt of those whose livelihood you provide, the withdrawal of your nearest and dearest, making it plain they have no sympathetic understanding of your life or appreciation of your work, the impertinent scorn of those who are untried in life's experiences? Have you ever dealt thus with any of your own friends, knowing perfectly well you have been deliberately lacerating their feelings? Do you know what it is when those you have confided in intimately, laying bare your heart to them, turn away from you and use their knowledge of you as a lash of criticism? Job was called to suffer like this, and it was by means of suffering that his God-given task was accomplished.

Do you feel you have plumbed the depths of darkness? There is one who has gone even deeper than you. No, not Job, but Jesus. As his work proceeded many went back and walked no more with him; they became disaffected and unsympathetic (John. 6:66). In the end our blessed Lord was absolutely alone.

19: 23-29

We have been thinking of Jesus as we have read Job's story.

Remember how Jesus' cry of anguish on the Cross gave way to the triumph of, 'It is finished!' and the peace of, 'Into your hands I commend my spirit.' The battle had been engaged, fought and won. So it is with Job, for from this point of climax the tension begins to ease, although there are yet many battles to be fought. Not by escapism, but in radical facing up to his grim circumstances, Job declares a faith that absolutely nothing can shatter, not even death itself.

All the morbid speculations about what happens to our earthly bodies in their inevitable disintegration, and what relationship there is between our resurrection bodies and our natural bodies, fade into obscure insignificance as Job utters these glorious words. Let time's destroying sway do its worst, and let every created power manipulate us and our circumstances as it may, in the end (and it is the end that counts), the man of faith knows that his mighty Redeemer and Vindicator shall appear before his eyes and all the hidden things will be made plain. Job says 'I know,' and this knowledge is his secret fortress in which he is safe from both men and devils. This is peace which the world can neither give nor take away.

Job has not come to this place of peace and confidence easily. Trace the progress in chapters 9:32-35; 10:7; 13:15-19; 16:19-21; 17:3. Job has reached this ground of confidence and says that 'in his flesh' he shall see God for himself, that is, on his side. The end of verse 27 reads, 'My heart yearns within me.' It seems to mean that he is longing for the day of vindication to come. How well we understand his desire. The last two verses are difficult. But take the last four words as they stand. They give a realistic background to life: 'There is a judgment'.

Job 20
Zophar: Words of Accusation

20: 1-29

Here is another discourse on the fate of the wicked with, of
course, a deliberate suggestion that Job is one such evil man
suffering already for his sins. It is quite clear that these men
have not really heard any of Job's words at all. They are
apparently quite incapable of receiving spiritual instruction.
So dead are they in their preoccupation with their own
spirituality that the glorious inspiration and revelation of Job's
words in 19:23-29 have made not one whit of impression.
Perhaps the final word about judgment stung them a bit and
produced the vitriolic diatribe of this chapter.

Sometimes we see the same utter insensitivity after a
searching sermon and, of course, similar bitter things are said.
It is so manifest that God is with Job, though mysterious in his
intention, that when these men insist that there is evil
inspiration in Job they must be coming very near to the
unpardonable sin, the final blasphemy for which there is no
forgiveness. They look and listen to the Spirit of God present in
Job's life and reject him. The sight of God's working has no
attraction whatever for them. It was the same with Jesus.
Religious men saw God in fleshly form before their eyes and
hated him.

To the man who lives in the light of eternity the triumph of
the wicked is short, even if his years go well beyond the allotted

span. But we have still to grapple with the undeniable fact that wicked men can in fact prosper all their earthly lives. On the other hand the truth of verses 4-7 stands as a terrible warning to those whose pride makes them fly in the face of God. Can there be any more devastating humiliation than to be forgotten?

Look at verse 22 and think of the frustration of those who have succeeded in their personal ambitions. Verse 26 tells of a strange, inexplicable fire that consumes. Verse 27 tells of the whole order of God's creation, heavenly and earthly, being against the evil-doer. Verse 29 sums it all up. God is not mocked, whatever a man sows, that he will also reap (Gal. 6:7).

Job 21
Why Do The Wicked Prosper?

21: 1-34

This chapter needs to be read as a whole in order to grasp the significance and depth of Job's words. He challenges his critics in verse 7 to give an explanation of evil in the world. Why do evil men prosper, often at the expense of the godly? It can only be because God either allows it or ordains it for his holy purposes. You cannot afford to pass superficial judgments or else, beguiled by immediate appearances, you will come to the wrong conclusion and end up with the Devil instead of God.

These men classed Job with the wicked, but look at verses 8-15. The wicked have their families; Job's is dead. Their houses are safe; Job's destroyed. Their cattle prosper; Job's are stolen. They have musical evenings; Job sighs in sorrow. They live lavish lives and die in a sudden coronary without the agony of illness endured by Job. They are openly irreverent, contemptuous of holy things and rebellious in the face of the Almighty, which was scarcely a description of Job's whole life. Now look down to verse 34 where Job simply says his friends do not know what they are talking about.

Job is more sure now that God is with him, and there comes to him a new detachment from men and their prattle. Having first of all been disappointed in his friends, he now begins to pity them, not least because their God-given opportunity of ministering to him is slipping away, and even if there is spiritual restoration they will never be able to recoup wasted hours! Job bids them listen quietly to his words, though he does not seem to hold out much hope of their learning (v.3). The tragedy of the unteachable is that they are most at home arguing theology, but it never touches their lives.

Now go on to the first half of verse 16. The prosperity of the wicked is not their own doing, for the issues of men's lives are in the hand of God alone. But this is not a simple concept. Look at verses 22-26. There seems to be no strict pattern as far as men can see. There is a mystery about life, as there is about evil, and we must learn to live with life and circumstances as they really are, and not as we view them through the rose-coloured spectacles of our particular theological or political ideology. The wicked prosper, the righteous suffer. But, sometimes the wicked suffer in this life and some godly prosper. Exactly. There is a mystery. Therefore judge nothing before the time (1 Cor. 4:5). Wait patiently upon God.

You may be exasperated that we can provide no slick answers to Job's particular problem or to the general problem of evil. But there is no slick answer, simply because God is bigger than we are and his ways are not ours. The final answer is of course God himself, who permits and ordains evil, though he himself is never in complicity with evil. There is no excuse for sin, nor is there ever justification for it, even though God may bring good to your life out of your wrongdoing. He will still judge your sins and you will pay a sore price for your transgressions.

SCENE THREE
Chapters 22-26

Job 22
Eliphaz: Slander

22: 1-5

This chapter begins the third cycle of speeches and replies (*cf.* 4:1 and 15:1). Job's pilgrimage has led him to the place of firm assurance in 19:25, and from that point he seems to be grasping the thought of purpose which he will express in 23:10: 'But he knows the way that I take; when he has tested me, I shall come forth as gold.' It is time to ask ourselves, 'What is my life for, in the will of God?' Our answer becomes the plumb-line by which all the other decisions of life are tested. You may react genuinely at this point, and cry that you would give anything to know just what God's will is. Do you mean what God will *give you* or what he would *ask of you?* There is quite a difference in these two attitudes!

Job did not know what God was doing with him. It is only now that he is beginning to realise that that is not really necessary or significant. God knows what he is doing with Job, and if his purposes are being evolved by this agonising process of life, then let it be so. We do not need to go seeking for some great thing to do; the demand of the plodding ordinariness of daily life is enough for most of us to bear. In any case who is able to say when he is doing 'spiritual' work and when 'ordinary'? Men will always say things such as verse 5. They do not like a man who is serenely confident in God.

In verse 4, Eliphaz asks, 'Is it for your piety that he rebukes you and brings charges against you?' Eliphaz' answer is in the negative and he concludes therefore that Job's present distress can only be because of sin (v.5). Eliphaz is in that class of religious men who are so spiritual that they are never able to give any credit or praise to any man (except perhaps themselves). When any work of God is well done and blessing ensues, they are quick to remind men, 'Of course, it is all of the Lord's doing.' They seem terrified lest any servant of God should have an exalted opinion of his own worth and make it their business to keep all such humble!

Verses 2 and 3 are of course a reminder that at best we are unprofitable servants. Job would say a hearty 'Amen' to that sentiment. But having regard to the opening chapters of this book, it is clear that God does have pleasure in Job's righteousness. God has a great appreciation and love for his servants, and we do well to emulate it (See Is. 62:3; Zech. 2:8; Mal. 3:17). Do we not also have a word of the Master that says, 'Well done, good and faithful servant; (Mat. 25:23). God is more willing to give praise than men. Men who are praiseworthy are seldom proud, for they are too conscious of the cost of service and grieve over their failures. It is the vain man, with nothing to his religion but words, who gets exalted with his own importance.

22: 6-22

This passage shows the extent to which some men are prepared to go in slandering the characters of God's saints with deliberate and groundless accusations. There is no doubt that Job's reasonings with these men, though apparently having no effect, had stung their consciences. There is a particular drive and point given by the Holy Spirit to truth on the lips of a godly man. Although thick-skinned men show no visible reaction, their inner hearts can be seething with rage and offended pride. When that happens, beware, for they will stop at nothing in their desire to descredit you. Eliphaz accuses Job openly of doing deeds of cruelty he had never done, and also of shamefully neglecting people he ought to have ministered to, which was also false. This is the essence of gossip which can set a whole neighbourhood into a turmoil of slanderous hatred of a man of God. Such tongues are set on fire by Hell (Jas. 3:6) and such hearts are in sympathy with Hell. But God knows. He will not hold such guiltless.

22: 23-30

Leave aside the horrible hypocrite Eliphaz, and take his words as a beautiful appeal, full of gracious promise, addressed to the broken sinner or saint who would wend his tearful way back to the Lord. Read verse 21, 'Submit to God and be at peace with him; in this way prosperity will come to you.' This is the way of blessing. In verse 23 the prodigal who abandons his sinning has not long to wait before the arms of the Father are round him. The long painful bit of returning from backsliding lies in the struggle to yield the self-will that first caused your departure. Verses 24-26 are an encouragement to lay your gold in the dust and the gold of Ophir among the stones of the brooks (counting them of little value), and the Almighty will be your gold and your precious silver. Then you will have your delight in the Almighty and lift up your face to God.' Where your treasure is there will your heart be also. Then follows prayer that is fellowship as well as intercession, and leads to fruitful service. There is much that is true here. What a pity that such a sermon was intended to beat Job down in humiliation rather than lift him up in tenderness!

Job 23-24
Cry From The Depths

23: 1-7

Here is one of the most thrilling chapters in the Book of Job. Job is counselled to submit to God (22:21), and he would do so if only he knew how (23:3). He reveals his secret heart and bares his inmost soul in all its struggles, and no sane man can doubt his earnestness. There is no easy religion to face life's realities. 'There is no reality without struggling,' (P. T. Forsyth).

To participate fruitfully in God's purposes will mean your way is often neither plain, obvious nor understandable. Shakespeare says, 'All the world's a stage,' but in fact you need to think of two stages, one above the other, with the action going on simultaneously. The earthly stage without the drama of the heavenly is quite beyond comprehension. The man of God has wars without and fears within; he is despised by men and tormented mentally (not morally) by the Devil. The pattern of his experience is often like Job's: 'Oh that I knew . . . *He* knows . . . *He* performs what is appointed for me' (vv.3,10,14). This is faith. Its value and worth are exactly what was paid for it. If you want quality you have to pay the price, not least in the realm of spiritual graces. There is no easy way to certainty, enjoyment and fruitfulness.

There is a suggestion in these verses that Job has tried to keep silence but feels he must cry out. The cry is not of rebellion, nor of a man trying to escape from God. This is not a perplexed man throwing over his once dearly-held faith. Job wants to get to God, not away from him. That tells a lot about the man. He has no intention of bickering with God, but longs for a reasoned explanation of what is happening to him. Do you not think that if God explained to Job what we read in chapters 1 and 2, the man would instantly consent and say, 'Be it unto me according to your word'? Of course he would. Job knows and trusts his God and is quite sure that the issue of a personal, face-to-face interview would be a renewing of his strength and a confirmation of his protested innocence. It is a happy man indeed who is as sure of his ground with God as this. It is given only to those who walk out in the open with their God.

23: 8-17

It is one thing to be led out into service on broad and deep dimensions, but another to be left there without any conscious awareness of God. You can scarcely help wondering if all your conflict is for no purpose. Job knows that God is always at work, but he can see no evidence at all relating this work to his life. But, God knows exactly what he is doing and Job is confident that when the smelting process is finished he will come forth as pure gold. It is not so much that Job interprets his sufferings as necessary refining, but that he claims that the process of God's dealings with him will reveal that right from the start he has been true and pure metal. Remember this glorious chapter comes to us by way of an answer to the criticisms of his 'friends'. This helps to explain the testimony of verses 11 and 12. It is this secret spiritual integrity of his life that is his anchor and peace now in the midst of storm. The word 'treasured' (v.12) reveals the genuineness of the man's whole attitude to God and his Word. He was no sermon-taster, nor did he evaluate any given passage according to the 'thrill' or 'blessing' of it. The Word was his food, sweet to his taste and absorbed to become part of his life. What a man! What a Christian, and Christ was not yet come in the flesh!

Wedged between two declarations of God's sovereign working in verses 10 and 12-13 we have the statement of human responsibility. But it is the sovereignty of God in his gracious purpose that is Job's strong tower, and not his own integrity. In verses 13, 14 there is tremendous assurance for the beleaguered saint. God will perform and complete his perfect purpose for this trusting man; but what of the last words of verse 14? The R.S.V. reads, 'He will complete what he appoints for me and many such things are in his mind.' Therefore Job says he is troubled or terrified at his presence. When he considers all God might yet have stored for him to do and suffer, he is filled with dread. Little wonder, for it is no small thing to be drawn into the company of a determined God of glorious power.

We can never say, 'Stop the world, I want to get off.' It is a sentiment we can understand, but it cannot be done. There is no escape. In a very real sense men are all trapped: either in the bondage of a world governed by the prince of evil, whose work is destruction, or safely trapped in the saving designs of God, whose will shall most surely be done with perfect completion. In Job's case the outworking of this work and will of God has led him into darkess that frightens him. He cannot see the next step, let alone the end of the road, but then he walks not by sight but by faith. Even though you cannot *see* the end you can *know* it. The life that is hid with Christ in God is safe, for ever and ever.

24: 1-17

Job returns to the theme of the careless prosperity of the wicked. In verses 1-11 he describes country life and in verses 12-17 city life. At the end of the last chapter, Job was fascinated by the grim realities of actual experience in which there are no signs of God at work and no intimations even to his saints of his near and comforting presence. He now asks, "Why?" After all, it takes real faith to face the fact of God's apparent non-intervention. Moffat renders verse 1, "Why has not the Almighty sessions of set justice? Why do his followers never see him intervening?" This is a pertinent question today. Why? Why? Why? This is Job's question.

What do the Scriptures reply? Consider Acts 1:7; Matthew 13:24-30; Matthew 24:36 and Hebrews 2:8-10. Take that last reference and ponder how it declares that *all has been* put under Christ, but in the earthly outworking we do *not yet see* all actually subdued. Time is part of God's plan and the patience of faith consists, in measure, in waiting for God to execute his designs. After all, since power belongs to him, no one else can bring his will to pass. This is not pietistic indifference to human need, but the beginning of worship. That in turn is the beginning of God-directed activity, which is the instrument of his saving purposes.

These verses are a description of man's inhumanity to man. What cruelty and indifference are portrayed! We who live amongst it in the great cities know it only too well. But we are also reminded of the Highland clearances in Scotland and every heartless commercial land transaction since. Some men will stop at nothing for gold. Take the first half of verse 12 as a text for a sermon on any great city. Go on to read of rebels against light, and the shadowy, secretive attitudes and activities that speak of evil. It is not a good sign to be a mystery, so that no one ever knows what you really think about things. There is an openness in true fellowship that is no denial of personal privacy, but rather a great safeguard against the subtle temptation to slip away from God and become in thought and action infected by the materialism and fascination of a sinful world.

24: 18-25

The first half of this chapter tells of human society riddled with evil, the strong and rich despising and persecuting the weak and poor. (You can be cruel by neglect as well as by positive action! *cf.* Luke 16:19ff.) The inhumanity of employer to employee is matched only by the inhumanity of employee to employee in strident self-interest. But everything will come out in the end! In verse 15 men say that no man will see, but verse 23b declares that God's eyes are on their ways. 'God is always near me, hearing what I say; knowing all my thoughts and deeds, all my work and play.' We call that a children's hymn!

Verses 18-20 should be prefaced by the words 'You say,' for Job is referring to his friends' statements about the prosperity of the wicked being swiftly judged. But in fact, God draws away the life of the mighty (wicked); no man can be sure of life. God gives men security, but they take it for granted. God's eyes are on all their ways. Here is not merely the permission, but the ordination of God in relation to evil. It takes real faith in a real God to face up to strong doctrine like this. In verse 24 emphasise the words 'like all others' and ponder the amazing impotence of evil men and things, when God decides their time has come. Prove me wrong if you can, says Job. Faith that waits in silence is deeper than that which rants and rails at the perplexities of life and experience. Real faith knows there is a God at work even when (indeed, especially when) there is no sign of him.

Job 25
Bildad: Mere Head Knowledge

25: 1-6

It is difficult to believe the venomous contempt inspiring this very short sermon of Bildad. Working on the assumption that Job is a worthless worm this man declaims in verse 4; 'How can a man be righteous before God?' Job never claimed to stand by his own merit before God. He simply said that the accusations of secret sin resulting in physical affliction were not true. Job would give glorious assent to verse 2: God makes peace. That is the glory of the full shining of the gospel. Only God can do this and it is wonder beyond expression that the God who is all-powerful and all-knowing (v.3) does in fact do this for worthless sinners. But Bildad did not need to teach Job to bow prostrate before a God of glory and power. We have seen that in the earlier chapters.

Bildad's knowledge of God was all in his mind, and bore no relation to the bleeding hearts of men. He liked a good discussion about religion, but would change the subject if it grew too personal. But Bildad had claimed the position of a 'spiritual' man and he had to keep up appearances by making some profound utterance. What he said was very true, *but it had nothing whatever to do with the situation or person in hand.* It was a sermon that missed the mark completely.

Make sure your religion never deteriorates into a mere pattern of evangelical conformity. Such religion is vain. After all, God is not a machine or a printed basis of belief. He is a Person with a heart and feelings who would have your company and your conversation, if you really have anything to say.

Job 26
Some Comfort You Are!

26: 1-14

In verses 2 and 3 we should, perhaps, change the question marks to exclamation marks, for Job is being mightily sarcastic, as if to say, 'That was a wonderful sermon and a great help to me in my weakness!' Verse 4 continues the biting sarcasm, 'Whose spirit spoke from your mouth?' It is as if Job is saying to Bildad, 'Could you possibly have thought out such profound precepts by yourself?' There are many Bildads who pass off other people's material as their own without any acknowledgement, and there are many Christians who are prone to try to teach those who taught them all they know. Bildad has spoken of a great God, and Job agrees with him, but then goes on to give utterance to the magnificence of God in very wonderful expressions. Job speaks of the active administrative God behind all the order of the universe. The earth is hung in space! Then in verse 10 the mighty ocean deep is bidden to keep its appointed place. But look at verse 9! Is it not wonderful to realise that this great God is not an ostentatious, extrovert showman? There is a hiding of his power (Hab. 3:4).

The lessons of the chapter are many. It is one thing to speak religious words but another to help people. Have you, in any sphere, been a help to anyone? To be a 'help' is a God-ordained calling (1 Cor. 12:28).

Verses 7-13 tell of God's power in all the created universe. In verse 13 'spirit' could be read as 'breath' or 'Spirit' and links with Genesis 1 where the Spirit broods on the face of the deep, and God's planned order of creation is fashioned. But when all is said and done, we are but discerning the fringes of his ways and the whisper or portion of his speech. When God thunders in the full chorus of his final triumph song, what will it be?

SCENE FOUR
Chapters 27-31

Job 27-28
Beginnings of Peace

27: 1-6

There is a suggestion here that Job pauses for a moment as if to give Zophar a chance to contribute to the continuing discussion, but the man has nothing to say and Job continues. We have now a long discourse in two parts, beginning at 27:1 and 29:1, and continuing to the end of chapter 31.

In Job's words here, there is a wonderful kindling of fire and conviction as he finally breaks free from the influence of his 'friends' who have been 'brain-washing' him in an attempt to extort a 'confession'. Had Job been of lesser spiritual calibre he might have capitulated under pressure, and accepted the interpretation of men rather than the inner persuasion of the Spirit of God concerning his life and experience. But the anchor of his soul is sure and steadfast, and his faith has a remarkable tenacity. He may not have known that at the instigation of God his life had been made a battlefield between God and Satan, but he was quite persuaded that God was in his predicament, and for a good and significant purpose. Men could not explain; but Job was persuaded (call it intuition if you will, or even a hunch, or the constraint of the Spirit) that what he was going through was neither for his chastening nor his perfecting. There was a purpose much bigger than Job, and if God chose to keep the details to himself he was perfectly entitled to do so. Furthermore, Job was prepared to stick to his claim of integrity and to his faith, though everything disintegrated around him. The issues were with God. That was safety enough for Job, and the beginnings of peace; but it had to be fought for.

27: 7-23

The faith and meek submission of Job and his long anguish do not in any sense take away his rugged manliness, as these verses show. Knowing that Job is right with God and in some significant way incorporated actively in the work of God, we see that those who lift up their accusing voices and hurtful hands against him are in fact against God. (Cf. Ps. 105:12-15; Is. 54:17). Those, pagan or religious, who deal falsely with God face an inevitable retribution. By way of exposition of verse 9 read Zechariah 7:8-14. Job is speaking here of the ultimate end of the wicked in a harvest of retribution, not necessarily reaped in this life, but yet reaped and gathered to the full individually, nationally and universally. Even though the wicked do seem to live with impunity in this life, the Bible declares there is an inescapable price to pay for the pleasures of sin. (Pro. 13:13-15; Jas. 1:15,16). The price may not be physical or material, but moral and psychological, and remember that our children inherit part of that legacy as well as our money!

In verses 11-12 Job says he will teach them about the hand of God in the things they see before their eyes every passing day. Why will men not learn? There are none so blind as those who refuse to see. They refuse to see because it is inconvenient and would demand a change in their way of life. These verses are blunt and chilling, not least the closing two verses where those who have dealt wrongly with God are seen to be cast off. The lesson is clear. Do not sell your soul to any, nor part with your inheritance in God for any of the bait of devilishly clever men.

28: 1-28

Some scholars say this chapter is not really part of Job's speech but a later addition to the story. It seems to be a quiet meditation on the nature of wisdom, and its tone, placid and serene, is a contrast to Job's other wrestlings after God and truth and peace. The immediate connection between chapters 27 and 28 is not very clear, and that is true also of chapters 28 and 29. Could it not be that Job, being now left free from the vain prattling of his friends, has time to ponder or brood over the facts of life? If this is so, then it is not surprising that the man who has plumbed the depths of agony also tastes the rivers of deep peace as he reflects on the wisdom of men and the wisdom of God. The sweep of this whole section is as follows: Chapter 27 discusses the fate of the wicked; chapter 28 speaks of the nature of wisdom; chapter 29 — wistful recollections of his past life; chapter 30 — the contrast of his present life; chapter 31 — the final assertion of his innocence and integrity.

Verses 1-11 describe the wonders of what man can do and find in the world by his skill and ingenuity. It is a theme which caused the poet Swinburne to say, 'Glory to Man in the highest! for Man is the master of things.' The falsity of such doctrine is demonstrated in our generation, with the world trapped in a fiendish web of danger of its own making. Far from mastering his works, man is hunted and haunted by them. Verses 12-22 ask simply where man's wisdom is getting him. It certainly has failed to bring him peace of heart. The hymn-writer says, 'My heart is pained, nor can it be at rest till it finds rest in Thee.'

The question in verse 20 is answered in verse 28. If any man would only be humble enough to come to terms with this God, how much more basic simplicity would be in his life. It does not mean life would be easy. Job's story makes that clear. But it would be free from the terror of nameless fears and the dread of manipulations by unknown powers of 'fate' and 'luck' and 'heredity'. Your times are in the hand of the God who understands and whose administration is that of perfectly co-ordinated power. He has a glorious purpose. To say, 'God knows,' is not an idle irrelevance. To the trusting heart it is peace.

Job 29-31
This Is My Life

29: 1-25

The whole of this wonderful chapter reveals the intense humanity of Job. In it he looks back over his life, and his thoughts linger wistfully on his earlier days. This is something we are all apt to do when present circumstances are difficult, and life is proving very demanding and perplexing. Unfortunately we are apt to view the past through rose-coloured spectacles, and our memories may have little relation to the actual facts of the past situation. Distance does often lend enchantment! Whereas our meditative recalling of the past usually consists of dwelling on all we possessed and all we received for our enjoyment, Job's recollection here is in fact of a life of service to others, a life of dignity and moral righteousness, a life of wise advice mingled with discipline that forbade familiarity. Granted Job was a man of affluence, but his associates were not only the rich, for the poor loved him. That is a testimony to the absence of snobbery and to the spiritual worth of a man whom God could trust with riches. Job recognised that all he possessed was the gift of God. That is plain from chapters 1:21 and 2:10. In the testing ground of wealth and comfort he was proved to be trustworthy. He was detached from his possessions and position, a sign of true greatness. He proved godliness with contentment to be great gain (1 Tim. 6:6).

Having qualified in the school of plenty, Job now has graduated to the school of poverty and suffering, where Jesus also sat (Heb. 2:10; 5:8). A superficial reading of the chapter could give the impression that Job's first love was the prominence of public life and praise. But read carefully and remember the long suffering of body, mind and spirit, and you will see that he is recalling the days when, under God, he was allowed to be servant to men in righteousness and holiness. That is the poignant note of verses 1-4. He thought, wrongly, that his days of holy service were over. In fact they were at their peak of spiritual significance.

In verse 5 we see the holy man to be a tender family man. The memory would be sore in his present loneliness. The next verses show Job at the seat of counsel and administration. Even the titled people paid heed to this man's words (10), as well they might. Mere rank is incidental if it is not borne by the good gold of character. The causes Job took up were unlikely to bring him fame or popularity (12-17). His advice was accepted (22) and rejoiced in, although some would no doubt be too proud to ask or take advice. Job himself was a true 'comforter' (v.25)!

30: 1-15

This whole chapter is set in sharp contrast to the previous one, and highlights the tremendous depth of perplexity and intensity of pain in Job's situation. You can imagine how often he must have asked why this had to be. He was in good company, if we think of Jesus in Gethsemane and in the darkness of the Cross when the Father's face was hidden. We need to remember this when we ask in prayer that we might be made like Christ.

Job here is the object of the derision of some arrogant, critical young folk (v.1) who, though their heads are full of religious theory, have not yet lived long enough to prove their reality in the grim testing arena of life. Far too many fruitless young Christians (who have still to prove that there is grace in their hearts) take delight in arrogant criticism of God's tried and trusted servants, to the point of the spitting of verse 10. They delight in their game of trying to knock Job's feet from under him, and like a noisome pestilence they are a blight on his life. They have a hurtful nuisance-value, and contribute nothing to God or man in prosperity or distress, for the simple reason that, apart from criticism, they have nothing at all to give. In due time even men see they are worthless and chase them out (5). These were young people who, when they were in straits, may have been helped by Job, but now that they do not need help they revile him. It does not seem to have occurred to them that they might now help Job. Some Christian leaders could tell you a lot about this kind of thing!

30:16-23

Job's distress is not only or even mostly caused by the attitudes of those younger than himself. There is an inner affliction of soul that is draining him of vitality, and the long continued days of travail are taking their toll (16). There is an aching, gnawing sleeplessness, and he wonders just how much more mere humanity can take of this dread, costly travail.

'I cry out to you,' says Job, 'but you do not answer' (v.20). His complaint is really very accurate, for he knows full well that God hears his cry and he is perplexed that there is no answer. In verses 20b-22 Job accuses and rebukes God, but there is no answering rebuke from God. It is not true to say that God looks on indifferently (20b), nor that God opposes Job; but, in the secret ways of God, he cannot be told this yet. In verse 22 Job speaks truth, for all his experience was in the hand and will of God. But it was not for nothing.

It was as Job grasped that his agonies were not in vain, but fraught with purpose and destiny, that he was able to stand them and continue. Even his wife, inspired by Satan, wanted him to curse God and die, saying that all was wasteful and needless. But Job chose to live, and suffer, and trudge on to the end. This is something you simply cannot explain to men of the world. They refuse to see it. Job, however, was like another great man who endured many trials because he saw the invisible (Heb. 11:27).

30: 24-31

We read these verses as a separate passage to make clear that though we speak of the spiritual *significance* of the suffering of God's saints, we do not in any way minimise the human *cost*. We believe that the more a man or woman is drawn into the deep workings of God, the more sensitive he becomes and the more his capacity for registering acute agony increases. It is not for nothing that our Lord is called, 'a man of sorrows and acquainted with grief' (Is. 53:3). We are surely told only a few of the occasions of his tears, for such weeping is private to God.

We sense the same about the great apostle Paul, who, for all his dynamic courage, was a man of feeling. Why else the wistful testimony that at the last he was left to stand alone (2 Tim. 4:16,17)? The great men of God, including the prophets of fire like Elijah, were, and are, all men of sensitive spirit. But there are few to whom you can open your heart as Job does here. It is almost a plaintive cry, 'Oh help me! Help me!' Job is not denying his faith or even dreaming of abandoning it, as some professing Christians do in time of distress. Job recalls that he has ministered to many in distress, but no one, not even God, ministers to him now (v.25 ff). Yes, Job is human, like Jesus. You can go to people like that when you are in need. They will not let you down.

31: 1-12

Job begins to give his testimony, and his words compare with those of Paul when he called God to be his witness (Rom. 1:9; 2 Cor. 1:23). He is not claiming sinlessness, nor is he denying any of the natural desires of the flesh; but he is claiming that in the full sweep of a truly human life he maintained a moral and spiritual integrity before God.

Job, taking very high standards as the requirement for a man of God, makes six claims, the first, in these verses, has to do with immorality.

In these days of the cult of permissive morality, which is no morality at all but an indulgence of unbridled and unprincipled passions, we need to be taught all over again that lust is a fire that rages and consumes. Yet it was not mere fear of consequences that restrained Job, but fear of God, which is a clean and healthy thing and a dynamic source of self-control. In verse 2 he reckons on the possibility of losing his portion of fellowship and service with God if he indulges in lewdness secretly or openly. In verse 1 with cold, calculating reason he makes a covenant with God regarding this sphere of natural human life. Then in verse 7 he speaks of the heart and will (and action) following after the roving, idle eye. Do you see the dangerous progression? Thoughts not disciplined; eyes lingering to the stirring of the imagination; and the blind blundering of the heart and life. 'If your eye offends you, cut it out.' If necessary it will help if you start by throwing away a lot of your paperback novels of filth masquerading as literature. Hell's fires need no encouragement.

31: 13-23

This section links with verses 31,32 and declares the second great sin of which Job was innocent. It is interesting that it takes second place only to lust. It is the sin of thoughtlessness, which is basically self-centredness. It issues in neglect. Never forget that Jesus told a story about a rich man who was so self-absorbed in work and pleasure that he ended up in Hell, where he was faced with the sin of neglecting the poor beggar who had sat at his gate for years.

How easy it is to become absorbed in 'I,' 'me,' and 'mine,' to the exclusion of all else. Job's words are very searching. 'If I, with my sufficiency have allowed any needy one within reach of me to go hungry and in need, let my arm drop from me, for I fear God.' Verse 23 seems to belong to this section, and Job declares he could not face God if he had so counted his own abundance as belonging to himself.

God is never impressed when people *leave* a lot of money, not even if they leave it to good or Chistian causes, for after all they have no further use for it. But God is very interested in a true and wise *stewardship* both of money and influence. A just dealing with people, friends and servants alike, giving them their rightful dignity as God-made creatures, is as vital as material ministration. It can actually be more demanding than a monetary donation. This man Job's religion was very practical.

31: 24-28

Job now claims freedom from two further sins: undue ambition (v.24,25) and secret idolatry (v.26,27). Both these warrant the just punishment of God the Judge, for they are both a denial of his rightful prior claim on heart and life.

Gold, with what it can buy in terms of comfort, pleasure and indulgence, to say nothing of social status, is the god many people worship. Some worship their money so much that they are afraid to part with it, and spend half their lives worrying about being in straits. The rat-race of 'getting on' in business is costing many a man his soul in these affluent and immoral days. We have heard of a young man in industry being rebuked by his superior (and forfeiting part of an increase in salary) because he kept aloof and did not co-operate with the group in their leisure pursuit of drunken leering about sex. Thank God for a suffering witness to righteousness!

The idolatry referred to immediately after 'getting on in the world' has reference to the worship of the sun or moon in Job's day, but is essentially connected with all 'secret' societies, including the secret signs, oaths and slithery handshakes of such organisations as modern Freemasonry. The cult of the initiated with its discrimination, suggestion and preference in an offence to God. God is light, and he would have men walk in the open.

31: 29-32

Verses 31,32 have already been discussed, but they have their place here also. Job claims freedom from the sin of bitterness or vindictiveness — that spirit of revenge that delights in the downfall of someone who has inflicted on you real or imaginary hurt or insult.

There is something in all of us that desires to 'take it out of' those who have crossed or disappointed us. It is only full-hearted forgiveness (as we ourselves have been forgiven by God) that can deliver the soul from bitterness. Scripture speaks of a 'root of bitterness' (Heb. 12:15) that grows to the corruption of the whole life and the infection of all contacts. One Christian with a cynical spirit, a nursed grudge, a jealous heart, a bitter attitude, can poison and virtually destroy a fellowship. Sometimes when you are battling in life and not making much headway, so that your trials are public, you become aware that your distress is giving someone perverse pleasure. He is glad you are down in the depths. Job was free from such a spirit in relation to his enemies, but we sometimes indulge it towards our friends and brother Christians, all the while preening ourselves on our superior spirituality. It is time we read 1 Corinthians 13.

31: 33,34

Job claims freedom from the sin of insincerity, or deceit, or hypocrisy. He speaks of the common practice of men, of putting a respectable face on disreputable actions. It is the facade of honesty that hides a persistent policy of corruption and evasion. This is the kind of man you dare not trust, because long practice of duplicity has so dulled his conscience that he has lost the sense of wrong.

Verse 34 speaks of those who live their lives not according to principles of honesty and conviction, but according to the opinions of men. Did I fear the crowd, asks Job, or did I walk in fear lest the 'best' families disapproved of me? Did I hold back from what my conscience before God indicated to be my true life, rather than displease or anger men? Verse 34 is an unfinished sentence. Job breaks off, for such a manner of life would be anathema to him. But it is true of many people. The fear of man brings a snare (Prov. 29:25). The Christian's testimony must always be that he will please God rather than men (Acts 5:29). If you consider Job's testimony as a whole, you will see his concern towards God and man (Acts 24:16).

When you are able to look God in the face you will look towards men with a new detachment and poise, and men will know you to be a man of God rooted in integrity. Whether or not they will *like* you is a different matter. Actually it is quite irrelevant.

31: 35-40

What a glorious climax to Job's whole defence and testimony! Left alone by God to suffer for a purpose not explained, and tormented by the tirade of human accusations and contempt, this man of God has given his testimony, affirming the moral and spiritual integrity of his whole manner of life. Here he stands and, for truth's sake, he can do no other. He has spoken, and will speak no more by way of controversy and argument with men. The words of Job are ended. The time for words is over, and he will wait now, with confidence, for God to speak. Job is confident he could and would face triumphantly any open debate on his integrity, and of course he is right.

Job, however, is still in measure confused as to whom he is dealing with. To resist the blandishments of Satan is both right and necessary, although men are not to rail wildly against the evil one (2 Pet. 2:11; Jude 9). But there is also a time to be discerned in which the action of true faith is rather quiet submission (1 Pet. 4:19). Job has yet to learn this radical submission and to regret many of his words. (Not that they were untrue, rather they were unnecessary. The saints of God are not required to justify themselves to men.) If Job was given a stated case, the Accuser could only say that his integrity was the cause of his conflict. God would agree, but he would also ask Job why he was unable to trust him in the dark. There is no answer to God's question. He is to be trusted in all his ways and methods. Lord, we believe; help our unbelief!

SCENE FIVE
Chapters 32-37

Job 32-33
Elihu: The Voice of Youth

32: 1-3

At long last Job's three friends are silent and it is a blessed relief to be free from their haggling, over-confident, graceless words. But their silence carries the same message as their words, for both are critical and contemptuous of Job because he has maintained his integrity before them. As far as they are concerned, Job is self-righteous, and, of course, you cannot reason with a man like that. Job's friends dismiss him, as it were washing their hands of the whole matter.

We need to remind ourselves of what we have seen all through our studies, that Job was not claiming sinlessness, nor seeking to stand with God on a basis of human merit. He was only claiming that as far as he knew his own heart he had maintained integrity and singleness of purpose before God. In all the arguments no one had shown him anything concrete to the contrary, and Job is now content to wait in silence until God himself will speak to explain the mystery of his life. He waits for God in the firm belief that none who wait on him shall be put to shame (Isa. 28:16).

Before God gets a chance to speak, the young man Elihu, full of indignation, rushes in to deliver himself of a long sermon lasting to the end of chapter 37. Job gets no chance to answer Elihu, and when God speaks in chapter 38, he takes absolutely no notice of him either, except to interrupt. Some scholars suggest this indicates that the Elihu section is no real part of the Book of Job. It seems better to say that Elihu should never have opened his mouth. It takes grace to know when to be silent, and after all, in chapter 37:23, Elihu confesses he does not understand God.

32: 6-22

This man seems to protest too much in his own defence to be genuine or sure of his ground. The passage extols Elihu! This is his justification for speaking, before he starts his sermon, but a true man of God does not need this, he just speaks and if he is true and speaks truth, the unction of the Spirit will empower his words. Elihu begins modestly, giving deference to age, but declaring truly that mere age does not fit a man to speak wisely. There are many old fools as well as young ones, and the old are often more rigid and unteachable in their folly than the young. But all who claim to speak by inspiration of God are not necessarily of God.

In verse 14 Elihu indicates he is taking a different ground against Job from that of the friends. In verses 21, 22 he claims he is quite free from the influences of men in his considerations: personalities do not come into it (but it is rather difficult to get away from Elihu's personality which looms very large). In verse 18 he claims he is constrained to speak by a spirit within him, but the description he gives indicates a compulsion rather than a constraint. This spirit works within him and he feels he will burst if he docs not speak. There seems to be more than a little of the intensity of spiritual adolescence here. In verse 18 he says: 'the spirit within me compels me.' He sounds 'spiritual', but this 'feeling' is not necessarily to be taken as guidance, although we make full allowance for human trembling when called of God to speak and act in his name. There seems to be too much of young Elihu in this for it to be of God.

33: 1-33

After another introduction concerning the virtues of Elihu, the man goes on with his speech to the end of the chapter. Then he immediately starts another speech! A third speech starts in chapter 36.

Here in verses 1-7 Elihu seems to take up Job's plea for a

human comforter and advocate in chapters 9:32-35; 16:20,21. He says in verse 6, 'I am human as you are,' and in verse 7 promises gentle treatment. This is very Christian in its sentiment, although it does not turn out to be so in practice.

Elihu goes on in verses 8-12 to rebuke Job, as the others had done, twisting his words to mean that Job has claimed *sinlessness*, whereas he had claimed *integrity*, quite a different thing. In verse 13 the advice is to submit to God instead of striving against him. But Job's one concern was to strive towards God not away from him or contrary to him. In any case, does the man who confessed, 'Though he slay me, yet will I trust him,' need to be preached at to submit to God? It is quite true that God is greater than man and is not accountable to man to explain all his actions (vv.12,13). but, nevertheless, God remembers our frame (Ps. 103:13,14). He requires us many a time to walk in the dark, trusting him absolutely, and that for long spells at a time, as Job has proved. Now, if God chooses to withhold explanations, it ill behoves men to give them. In such distress, tears of fellowship with suffering are far more profitable than lectures in harsh theology.

In verses 14-23 the theme is God's patient dealings with his children. By speech and actions he seeks to lead them in the way everlasting. In verses 14, 15 we have the whispered guidance of God repeated in mercy, as in the story of the young Samuel. Guidance is seldom by strange vision, but usually by the quiet, inward intimation of the Spirit. If that is not heeded, God speaks with the voice of afflictions. Elihu declares in verse 19 that God speaks by sickness, and again that he speaks by sending someone (like Elihu?) to interpret the message of God's dealings. All this is very true. God may need to lead us down into the depths in order to prevent us from making a mess and a failure of our lives. His actions, therefore, though stern, are the workings of grace and love. It is love that will seek us even by pain, if only it can finally win us and our loving response.

The last section of the chapter, verses 24-33, is a great sermon on the restoration of backsliders. This is the end of all God's dealings with his own children, to bring them close to himself. God has found and provided a ransom or atonement to heal the fellowship that was broken. Verse 25 speaks of a physical renewal and freshness. When you come out from under a spritual cloud, even your voice is different. Not least is the change manifest when you lift your voice in prayer, for you see again the face of your God and are glad.

Verses 26 to 28 constitute a tremendous expression of the care God has and the value he sets upon an individual soul. Does it not amaze you how much bother God takes with you, persisting in his gracious disciplines even when you have sickened of yourself and would fain give up? Elihu's last words in the chapter are cold, as if he knew the doctrines of grace with his intellect but did not feel them with his heart. By contrast God feels pain when he beholds human sin and brokenness (Gen. 6:6).

Job 34
Elihu: The Righteous God

34: 1-12

Elihu launches into his second sermon and it seems certain he now has an audience extending to considerably more than Job's three friends. The young eloquent philosopher and theologian is getting quite a kick out of addressing himself to the wise and knowledgeable (v.2), and he appeals for the exercise of discernment and discrimination among 'ourselves' (v.4). Young Elihu takes his place among the grey-beards of wisdom. We recall hearing of a wise man commenting on an aspiring cleric, 'He would love to be up among the angels, if he knew who the angels were!' Elihu felt it best to cultivate the 'big' men rather than Job. How wrong he was!

In verses 5-9 he states what *he* thinks is Job's complaint, namely that he has been unjustly afflicted by God and that his holiness has been unrewarded. This is scarcely true, for while Job has all along confessed and wrestled with the apparent contradictions of his faith, he has really kept the ground from which he started and still has not charged God with wrong (1:22). But he could not rest in an unthinking attitude, and he has grappled intellectually and spiritually to come to a reasoned apprehension of God, his will and his workings. It is only by the wrestling of faith (Job does not doubt God, he simply cannot understand him at present) that we come to the peace of such verses as Romans 8:28; Philippians 1:12; and

Genesis 28:15; 50:20. The statement of Elihu in verses 10-12 is in fact the ground of all our confidence. Shall not the Judge of all the earth do right (Gen. 18:25)? It is a pity that knowledge had not created a humble spirit in him.

34: 13-30

There are too many wonderful words here to expound them all. The theme is the absolute sovereignty of God in righteousness, power and knowledge. If we read in from verse 10, we have first the righteous God who causes men to reap that which they have sown. His authoritative rule over all is unquestioned (v.13). God is impartial and no respecter of persons (v.19). There are no secrets from this God, and he is always at work executing righteous judgment among men and nations (vv.21-25). His providence is the defence and shelter of those who trust him, so that they taste peace that passes all understanding (v.29). He is a God with whom there is no variation or shadow of turning (Jas. 1:17). This is why God is a mighty rock in whose unchangeable righteousness we can trust even when all of life surges in inexplicable mystery.

34: 31-37

Elihu now rounds on Job in a swift and vicious application of this sermon. In v.33 he pleads with the fervour of an evangelist (and using similar expressions), 'You must decide, not I.' He says to Job, 'You know in your heart that I am speaking the truth about you!' But that was the trouble: Job's conscience was clear. In fact these words of Elihu have a sinister ring to them. It is not only God who is concerned about our sin. Our sins are Satan's stock-in-trade, and the tinge of bitterness in Elihu's words here does not breathe the spirit of the Comforter whom God sends to convict of sin (see John 16:8-11). 'Oh that Job might be tested to the utmost, for answering like a wicked man . . . He multiplies his words against God' (v.36). But Elihu is simply trying to emphasize the superiority of his theology over that of Job — and his own superiority as well. Paradoxically, that is an expression of his own insecurity before the mystery of God's dealings with the man who sits listening to him. Elihu did not really care for Job with a true, Christ-like pastoral care. Nor was that the result of his youthfulness (although youthfulness can be very uncaring). It was because he had a heart which had never been melted to care for the Lord's people. Beware the symptoms!

Job 35
Elihu: Sinful Man

35: 1-16

Elihu now deals with what he thinks is Job's second complaint, namely that his holiness has been unrewarded. In fact Job has not said this, although he has said something similar to it. All along Job has declared that his rightousness has not delivered him from suffering, and this is in full accord with the New Testament, where the godly are told plainly what it will mean in this world to be faithful to God. Compare Matthew 10:21-25; Mark 10:30; John 15:20; 16:2; 2 Timothy 3:12; 1 Peter 4:12-14. The nearer you are to the Captain the more you are the target for the archers! Elihu would never have understood Paul's teaching that Christians suffer in fellowship with Christ (Col. 1:24). Have you?

In a sense Elihu is more concerned here with the vindication of God's sovereignty than God is. It is true that God is ultimately unaffected by men, but that does not mean he is indifferent to men. Look at the Cross and you will see that! Job's cry has been that of a trusting soul asking where God comes into the complicated agonies of his life. Elihu's answer is that God is transcendent, far above the wrestling of human experience. By itself, that is cold comfort. It speaks of a God of glory and power who works his sovereign will. But the Gospel speaks of a God who put on mortal flesh and dwelt among us. Where is God in all the confusion of your life? Right in it with you.

Elihu accuses Job of pride because he thinks it makes some difference to God whether he lives a holy or a sinful life. Elihu seems to find in God's sovereignty a cancelling out of moral values. He suggests that human sin may affect human beings, but that God is far above such mundane trivialities. You cannot but wonder what kind of life Elihu lived. If you set God high enough in detached absoluteness, you are apt to forget about Him completely.

Verses 9-13 seem to suggest the theme of men's complaint at unanswered prayer. Elihu criticises them for not saying, 'Where is God my maker who gives songs in the night?' (v.10) Elihu had never experienced the dark night of the soul when, after spiritual service, desolation can possess mind and heart and even will. What of our Lord's words in the Garden about the cup passing from him, or his deep loneliness on the Cross? There was no answer. Agony and death had to be endured if the work was to be accomplished. What lessons are here for those with hearts to understand!

Verses 14-16 are an exhortation to trust God in the dark, because in fact His righteous judgments are at work among men. Job had already come to that place of trust in chapter 23. In verse 15 Elihu accuses Job of being encouraged in his complaints because God has been far too gentle and kind to him. Such thoughts make you long for God's intervention to blast this presumptuous youngster who prattles so much with his theoretical religious precepts that have still to be put to the test of adult daily experience!

Job 36-37
Elihu: The Transcendent One

36: 1-15

These are the introductory verses to Elihu's final speech and it is obvious that he is carried away by a sense of his own impressiveness. He takes to himself the place of God's spokesman. As the self-appointed counsellor of tried and proven saints he claims for himself a vast range of knowledge. It is not very clear in verse 4 whom Elihu refers to as being 'perfect in knowledge'. It looks very much as if he means himself. If so, he would not be the first person to act upon such a confused notion.

Leave Elihu and think of his sermon. Chapters 36, 37 deal with the mighty works of God. This is Elihu's idea of power, a show of strength. It is certainly the strong arm of God he emulates in dealing with poor, battered, assailed Job. There is a time for the rod of God to be wielded in rebuke of sin, but there is a time when gentle comfort must take precedence. In fact greatness and gentleness go together, for it is God's gentleness which makes a man great. Did you know that? (2 Sam. 22:36)

This is a great passage. Perhaps, even in his misery, Job could thrill to it, for it exalts God and shows his wonderful ways. Verses 5, 6 describe a mighty and gracious God and a trustworthy providence. Verses 8-10 tell of the education that comes through chastisement. Note the opening word of v.11.

Not all benefit from God's dealings with them. Some never ask what God is saying to them. But notice too that verse 11 falls down in the case of Job. (Elihu, of course, like the others, believed Job to be a disobedient backslider.) Affliction reveals false religion, for unreal Christians do not pray when God hems them in.

36: 16-33

These verses are difficult to understand, even in a modern translation. The section beginning with verse 26 runs on into the next chapter and is a description of the greatness of God displayed in nature, inspired by the evidences of a great thunderstorm then breaking. Verses 16-21 seem to be Elihu's interpretation of Job's experience. He declares that God saw Job's prosperity to be a snare to him and delivered him from it. If only he had been humble enough to submit, the trial would have been short, but, because Job had been resentful like the wicked, his fate has been long and sore.

We need to remember God's testimony to Job's character in the first two chapters, and also to recall the swift ruthlessness of the tragedy that smote the man in removing wealth, family and health in swift succession. We know that under pressure he uttered many extreme things, incited by the provocation of his 'friends'. No doubt God will call him to answer for the bitter words of his complaint. But this man Elihu is a thorough-going accuser, and that is satanic work. He crushes in order to destroy, whereas the rebukes of God have as their end the healing and raising up of the man into fellowship and service.

Verses 22-25 constrain our hearts to bow before the mighty righteousness of all God's dealings with us. But Job had expressed this very sentiment away back in chapter 23, when he declared that God knew the way he was being made to walk in, and that he was content that it should be so. Do you see, looking back over Job's story, how his friends never gave him credit for anything, nor did they make any allowances for factors in the situation they did not know? Such a spirit is not of God.

37: 1-24

Read in from verse 26 of the previous chapter and you will

sense the mighty music of these verses which speak so fully and with such awe concerning the God of nature. All the moods and movements of creation declare with unequivocal voice, 'The hand that made us is divine.' Job is told to consider well the thundering voice of God and to bow in his presence with fear (v.14). Twice over, in 36:26 and 37:23, Elihu declares that God is incomprehensible and yet he presumes to declare emphatically all that God is thinking about Job and doing with him! There seems to be a contradiction in this man's whole religious attitude, and it would have been better for him to have joined with Job and confessed the mystery of God's workings.

God's ways are not men's ways, and God's purposeful thoughts are on a different plane from the self-centred thoughts of men. His ways are past finding out and we must never presume to think that we completely understand all he is doing. He is a God of many surprises, who brings his gracious will to pass in ways that are astounding to men. Think of how God brought his purpose of redemption to victorious climax on the gallows of Calvary. But there was no need to be baffled, for all was in fact working according to a perfectly conceived plan, whereby the forces of Hell were being confronted by their mighty Conqueror. It was the same with Job, for God had chosen Job's life as the battlefield where Satan, though permitted full scope for his designs, would be put to shame and flight by a man's faith. Whatever God ordains or permits, we can be sure there is deliberate purpose in it. True faith consists in taking a good hard look at the evidences of our circumstances, and then resting on the Word and purpose of a gracious God, even although no explanation is forthcoming. That is what Job had to do and that explains his deep wrestlings of spirit.

SCENE SIX
Chapters 38-41

Job 38-39
The Voice of God

38:1-3

The manifestations of nature described by Elihu have built up into a whirlwind, out of which God now speaks to Job, answering Job's final request in 31:35. Verse 2 could apply to Job. But following our interpretation in previous chapters and having regard to God's words in 42:7, we conclude that he is here dismissing young Elihu as having been an unfortunate and unnecessary intrusion into a deep and significant situation. The link in sequence would then be from 31:40 to 38:1 and 3. Note carefully that although God speaks, he does not in fact give Job an explanation of his sufferings, but rather leads Job to a contemplation of his God's almighty Person and power. In him alone is peace found.

Think back over the whole of the Book of Job. Apart from the first two chapters, the stage has been held by men and the interchange of men's words to no real profit. From this we must learn that there is a time to cease from argument and wait for God to make things plain. Neither Job nor any of his friends was vitally aware of the spiritual dimension and significance of what was going on, and therefore many of their theological words, though true, were inapplicable. We know from the introductory chapters that Satan's assault was not primarily against Job as a person, but against the work committed to him. Job was distracted by men and perplexed by the silence of God until he was a pitiful sight, crushed down in abject misery, wilting under the tongue-lashes of 'Christian' men. Then God speaks, calling Job to stand upon his feet that he might reaffirm his essential human dignity. God is concerned to lift up his servant's head, for he has no pleasure in the humiliation of his chosen instruments.

38: 4-38

God's answer to Job's perplexity was not to give an explanation of all that had been happening to him, but rather to give a picture of the might and majesty of God in the wisdom and power of his Kingdom. This section deals with inanimate creation. God declares he is omnipotent, omniscient and omnipresent. He speaks in verses 4-11 of the earth and sea; in verses 12-15 of the dawn; in verses 16-21 of the secret things; in verses 22-30 of the weather; in verses 31-38 of the universe.

The lesson of all this is simply that we must learn to let God be God. We are so besotted with pride that we constantly make man and ourselves the centre of the whole ordered universe. But verse 26 tells us to remember the vast stretches of God's activity hidden from us as to their purpose, because we are too limited to comprehend it. It is almost as if God were inviting Job to take over the administration of the world and order it with the same competent power as he has done.

When you think of your situation in that light, are you not more than willing to allow God to continue to order your affairs, although he gives you no time-schedule of explanation for every day? Of course God will do his will with you, whether you like it or not. But it is much less painful when you yield willingly. Look at verse 11 and apply its message to the storms and satanic attacks in your own life. 'This far and no further,' is the command of God. He knows exactly what you need and what you can stand.

38: 38-39:30

The great God who rules the created order of things rules also in the animal kingdom. Here, as in the previous passage, we have a long series of questions addressed to Job, all of them emphasising the limitation of his person and power. The picture here is of a God who is present and active in every sphere of life, with every thing and person safely controlled by the government of his almighty power. The power of God is not indiscriminately let loose in blundering collision and shattering destruction. His power is yoked to his purpose and there is intelligent administration of all things and people. To men's eyes and even to Christian hearts the situation may seem to be utterly confused, but to consent to such a thought is to accuse the Almighty of indifference or even waste. If God watches over a single sparrow so that it does not fall without his knowledge, will he send his child into sore conflict for no purpose?

No one can deny that there are mysteries in God's ways. Can you explain the ways of animals, for example, in their long flights of migration, or their hibernation throughout winter? Can you explain why some do one thing and some another? No, you say, I am not God. Exactly! But we act like God at times, as if everything had to be explained to our complete satisfaction before it could be allowed. Are you not ashamed of all your questionings, complainings, and fretful lack of submission in the face of God's dealings with you?

Job 40-41
His is the Power

40: 1-5

Job has been questioning the ways of God with him, but now that God has spoken of his matchless power and inscrutable wisdom, Job will speak no more. Having heard the voice of God, Job will no longer vex himself about the methods of God but will yield to the Person of God. This is very wise, because, as we have seen, the explanation of Job's life and experience is not found on the human level at all, but in the heavenly realm, which at present we know only in part and see only in a mirror dimly (1 Cor. 13:12). The time is not yet come for the hidden things to be made plain. Much of our life will never be explained to us until we take our place in eternal service within the completed plan of God's redemption. That is why we must learn to wait upon the Lord, and to wait in patient possession of our souls, rather than in vexation and questioning (*cf.* Lk. 21:19).

God's words to Job are painfully direct, but already they are leading Job towards peace, the kind of peace that will be a strong tower of safety. In verse 4 Job is abased but not humiliated, and his words might be rendered, 'I am insignificant,' for this is not a confession of sin. But is Job of small account? Has not God boasted of Job? Has not God's case been committed to Job's safe-keeping in face of the taunts of Satan? Yes! But these are the very things that make a man feel his nothingness and compel him to bow in adoring worship.

40: 6-14

The atmosphere of this confrontation of Job by Almighty God is that of a whirlwind. It must have been awesome both in sight and sound. We cannot help wondering where the other four men are and what they are doing. Certainly they are being completely ignored by God. They are no longer relevant to his purpose, and they are not to be considered on the same level as Job. God does not question Job's integrity. It was God who first emphasised it in chapters 1:8 and 2:3. But he challenges him for questioning the wisdom and rightness of his ways. In verse 8 Job is asked if he has been trying to make God appear to be in the wrong. Now, says God, in the realm of moral issues, can you by the majesty of your person subdue evil? If you can do that, I will praise you, for your own right hand can save you (v.14).

Why is God speaking in such terms to his exhausted, suffering servant? It is because, through these religious men, Job has been bludgeoned by Satan into being completely absorbed and overwrought by the facts of his circumstances. The only thing God can do to deliver him is to tell aloud the glories of his being and works. Lift up your eyes, Job, there is a God in Heaven, a living God, who works his perfect designs on earth by using every power, whether good or evil, to do his will!

There is no ultimate power but God's power, and in its executive decisions there is never confusion or mistake but always perfectly balanced wisdom and skill. Do you see how Job's heart has been eased away from its true rest and trust by the verbal and emotional battles of these many chapters? Look back to chapters 1:20-22 and 2:10. It is to that same place but with deeper calm that Job is now being brought after the evil day of Satan's temptation.

40: 15-24

Job is now compared very unfavourably with an unknown creature, the behemoth (possibly the hippopotamus!). The burden of this passage and the next chapter seems to be to bring home to man his limitations. This mighty beast does not even tremble when the rivers are violent and overflow, but for all his strength he is subject to God who made him. This picture of strength accentuates Job's sense of weakness, and God does this because it is when they are weak that God's servants are really strong. It is then that they lean heavily in utter trust upon their God, leaving the disposing of their ways entirely in his hands without questioning his actions. This is the peace that enables us to stand in the evil day (Eph: 6:13).

Lest we are seduced away from the ground of peace, we must learn true discernment of the powers that bear upon our lives. When life brings us to the point of useless despair, as Job's experiences did in chapter 7:15,16, we must question the nature of our affliction. Is it from God and to be submitted to, or is it from the Devil and to be resisted? (*cf.* Jas. 4:7 and 1 Pet. 5:5-9). But discernment to try the spirits does not come easily; it involves the whole attitude, disposition and desire of your life unto God. It is only those who are growing up in grace who increase in knowledge and discernment (see Heb. 5:11-6:3).

Was not Job a man of stature in the things of God? Yes! But he either forgot, or was unaware of, the satanic element in holy warfare. That is to omit a fundamental factor. But perhaps there are realms of service where even the mightiest saints have to walk in deep darkness, in experiences of anguish that may be told to none, and in isolation so deep that they feel that even God has left them alone. There may be times when that is the only explanation for our experience. But, God knows the way he takes.

41: 1-34

This creature leviathan, seems to be the crocodile, or some similar water animal of great fierceness and strength. If men have any sense they keep clear and do not interfere with such a creature. Why then do men seek to interfere with the strong providences of God who alone controls the fierce beasts and subdues their fury (v.10)? This kind of passage exalts God and punctures the pride of man who struts about as if he were master of all things and monarch of all he surveys. In fact, apart from God, he is a puny, frightened creature, trapped by the social chaos he has helped to create by his facile optimism and narrow earth-bound thinking. There is nothing so pathetic as a man who has no element of the eternal in his thinking about life. Dust he is and to dust he shall return, and the world will forget about him so quickly that his insignificance will be confirmed.

While mortals rise and perish, God endures unchanging on. God is no man's debtor. All that is under the heavens is his (v.11). He made us, we are not our own and were never meant to be our own. It is only the folly of our pride that makes us want to be independent. It is not only safety but fulfilment that is found in submission to his wise will. Think of the summons to consecration in Romans 12:1,2, but remember that you are making an absolute offering of your whole person to be used in whatever way God ordains for his glory and his pleasure. Can you trust him? Even if your lot be like Job's? You will not be the loser!

Epilogue
Chapter 42

Job 42
Delivered and Restored

42: 1-6

The Lord has spoken to his servant Job in words which declare his majesty and power. Now the servant opens his mouth to speak to his God. That such conversations are possible is one of the wonders of God's grace. All his dealings with us are designed to bring us to himself, that we may open our hearts and speak to him. This is something we can do even when we are extremely conscious of our faults and failures, as Job is here. God is not concerned to hold things for ever against us, when we give evidence of true penitence. It is a work of Satan to shackle the mind and emotions to the past, when in the present God draws near to us in blessing.

Job's first word here is an expression of confidence in his God. 'You can do everything, and no purpose of yours can be withheld from you.' God knows what he is doing with you, and he is able to bring you through it all to his perfect conclusion.

Job now confesses that his restless struggling with his situation was in fact lack of faith. This does not mean we should not grapple with our situation, seeking to understand it more fully in the light of God's will for our life and service, but we must not allow such wrestlings to hurt us to the extent that they exhaust body, mind and spirit. We must learn to rest, even to relax, in God. He is the mighty Worker, and when we waste our precious energies in futile mental and emotional torture we are left in a condition of exhaustion, so that when God calls us to action we are impotent and even incompetent. We need to remember that!

Remember that Job is now answering God. He is beginning to realise that it is *God* to whom he has been speaking. We are all ashamed at times of the petulant, ill-considered words we address to the Lord, and it is good that we should acknowledge it. God likes honesty. Verses 5, 6 are moving. Job says he had *heard* of God but now he has *seen* him face to face. There is a new spiritual immediacy about Job's life of faith, and as a result he speaks the words of verse 6, 'I despise myself, and repent . . .' It can hardly mean that Job despises himself totally, for God has testified to his saintliness and character. God has entrusted holy service to Job, and has triumphed against Satan in Job's life of faith. It seems then that Job means that he cancels out his 'self', content to disappear and be no longer significant, that God may be all in all. That links Job with John the Baptist's confession, 'He must increase but I must decrease,' (John 3:30) and with Paul's declaration, 'I die daily' (1 Cor. 15:31). This is the death that leads to life, and the corn of wheat which in dying brings forth a harvest (John 12:24).

We must hold these verses in the light of all that has gone before, remembering all the humiliating accusations of the 'friends'. Men had left Job lying in misery, but God leaves him standing like a man and worshipping like a saint, as he in fact is.

42:7-9

Here is the vindication of Job's spiritual integrity that we have been longing for right through the book. Four times over God refers to Job as, 'My servant', and Eliphaz and his friends are shown to have been hindrances rather than helps. Young Elihu of the many words is still ignored. For all his fine theology he seems to have had no real part in the situation. God had marked down against them their harsh, vicious attacks on his servant — attacks launched when the man was already paying a deep price of suffering in the spiritual work committed to him by God. God was angry, very angry, and all that these men had done to Job was reckoned as having been done against the God himself (*cf.* Zech. 2:8,9).

They repented, but there was no easy way back to favour with God. They had to go humbly to the man they had wronged so spitefully and they were accepted *for Job's sake!* The suffering servant becomes both the mediator and intercessor. What a vindication of Job before the faces of the men who had slandered both his person and his work!

There was no unseemly pride about Job in this matter, nor did he lord it over his erstwhile detractors. Self had been cancelled out, and Job prayed for these men who had been such enemies and who had used him so spitefully. The excruciating suffering he had endured had wrought in him a truly Christ-like spirit. That is the final answer not merely to men, but to Satan, whose contemptuous mockery of God's grace started this whole mighty epic of the triumph of grace in a human life when everything was against it.

42: 10-17

The final picture of Job is of a man turned from his own misfortunes to the work of intercession for others. His praying for his friends was not the *ground* of his deliverance but rather the *crown* of it, and he was restored or reinstated to his life of abundance. Had Job fallen short here he would have been the loser, for he would not have known that exquisite fellowship with God which is the blessing of those who are God-like. To forgive those who have wronged you is negative if it remains there. To receive them back to fellowship and privilege is better, but to pray for them as well is the seal on the whole gracious work.

We can but hope that Job's three friends were brought to a sensitive knowledge of the God of grace, so that their future dealings with men in the name of God would have a tender touch of humanity about them. Poor Elihu is still forgotten, but he was a young man, and a few more years of real experience of life would fashion his theoretical theology into practical grace and understanding.

We are not surprised at the bounty of God in Job's life with which the story ends, but 'things' did not mean all that much to Job. He did not despise them and no doubt he stewarded them for God's glory, but he did not *need* them. Verse 11 casts a shadow. They had little time for Job *during* his agony, but now they flocked around with prattling words of sympathy, as if to say, 'What a hard time the Lord has given you!' Job would not discuss things with them. They would not understand. It is those who suffer who alone can understand. That is why deep friendships are often few, but they are very precious.

Job lived a long time after all this and he died a ripe old man with a full harvest that would be his crown to cast at his great Redeemer's feet. We close with Job's own words 'I know that my Redeemer lives . . . and after my skin has been destroyed, yet in my flesh I will see God.'

Well done, good and faithful servant. Glory to you, O good and faithful God of all grace, for your grace brings us safe to the end!